A PRIMER OF VISUAL LITERACY

The MIT Press   Cambridge, Massachusetts, and London, England

A PRIMER OF VISUAL LITERACY

Donis A. Dondis

The lines from Carl Sandburg's The People, Yes (New York: Harcourt, Brace and Company, Inc., 1936) quoted on pages 5 and 51 are reprinted with permission of the publisher.

This book was designed by the MIT Press Design Department.
It was set in IBM Composer Univers and printed and bound by Halliday Lithograph Corp. in the United States of America.

First MIT Press paperback edition, August 1974
Second printing, January 1978
Third printing, December 1978
Fourth printing, November 1979
Fifth printing, June 1981

Library of Congress Cataloging in Publication Data
Dondis, Donis A
  A primer of visual literacy.
  Bibliography: p.
  1. Art—Technique. 2. Composition (Art) I. Title.
N7433.D66   001.55'3   72-11579
ISBN 0-262-04040-9 (hardcover)
ISBN 0-262-54029-0 (paperback)

Per Sorella Borsetta con Cuore

Priscilla Anne Karb

San Sopostibi, 1973
D. D. and M. C.

PREFACE

If the invention of movable type created a mandate for universal verbal literacy, surely the invention of the camera and all its collateral and continually developing forms makes the achievement of universal visual literacy an educational necessity long overdue. Film, television, visual computers are modern extensions of the designing and making that has historically been a natural capability of all human beings and now seems to have been isolated from human experience.

Art, and the meaning of art, the form and function of the visual component of expression and communication, have changed sharply in the technological age without a corresponding shift in the aesthetic of art. As the character of the visual arts and their relationship to society and education has shifted dramatically, the aesthetic of art has become more fixed, anachronistically locked into the notion that the primary influence in the understanding and forming of every level of visual message should be based on noncerebral inspiration. While it is true that all information, input and output alike, must be strained at both points through a net of subjective interpretation, this consideration alone would make of visual intelligence something of a tree falling noiselessly in an empty forest. Visual expression is many things, in many circumstances, to many people. It is the product of highly complex human intelligence of which there is pitifully little understanding. To open up a broader knowledge of some of the essential characteristics of that intelligence, this book proposes to examine the basic visual elements, the strategies and options of the visual techniques, the psychological and physiological implications of creative composition, and the range of media and formats that can be appropriately categorized under the heading of the visual arts and crafts. This process is the beginning of a rational investigation and analysis designed to expand the understanding and utilization of visual expression.

While A Primer of Visual Literacy does not propose that simple or absolute solutions exist for the control of a visual language, clearly the central reason for its exploration is to suggest a variety of methods of composition and design that recognize the diversity of the structure of the visual mode. Theory and process, definition and exercise, stand side by side throughout the book. One aspect without the other cannot lead to the development of methodologies to achieve a new channel of communication, which can ultimately, like writing, expand the means for human interaction.

Language is simply a communication resource, natural to man, which evolved from its pure and basic aural form into literacy, reading and writing. The same evolution must take place with all the human talents involved in previsualization, planning, designing, and making visual objects, from simple toolmaking and crafts to the creation of symbols, and, finally, to picture making, once the exclusive province of the trained and talented artist, but through the incredible capability of the camera the option of anyone interested in learning a few mechanical rules. But what of visual literacy? Mechanical replication of the environment alone does not make a good visual statement. To be in control of the amazing potential of photography, a visual syntax is necessary. The advent of the camera parallels that of the book, which originally placed a premium on literacy. "Between the 13th and the 16th centuries, word order substituted for word inflection as a principle of grammatical syntax. The same tendency occurred with word formation. After printing both tendencies accelerated greatly and there was a shift from the audible to visual means of syntax."* To be considered verbally literate, one must learn the basic components of written language: the letters, words, spelling, grammar, syntax. What can be expressed with just these few elements and principles in the mastery of reading and writing is truly infinite. Once in command of the skill, any individual can produce not only an endless variety of creative solutions to verbal communication problems but also a personal style. The structural discipline lies in the basic verbal structure. Literacy means that a group shares the assigned meaning of a common body of information. Visual literacy must operate somewhat within the same boundaries. It can be no more rigidly controlled than verbal communication, no more and no less. (Who would want it controlled rigidly, anyway?) Its purposes are the same as those that motivated the development of written language: to construct a basic system for learning, recognizing, making, and understanding visual messages that are negotiable by all people, not just those specially trained, like the designer, the artist, the craftsman, and the aesthetician. Toward that end, this book will attempt to present exactly what its title proposes, a basic handbook for all visual communication and expression, a survey of all the visual components, a common body of visual resources with an awareness and desire to recognize the areas of shared meaning. I hope it is, as promised, a primer.

*Marshall McLuhan, "The Effect of the Printed Book on Language in the 16th Century," in Explorations in Communications, Edmund Carpenter and Marshall McLuhan, eds. (Boston, Mass.: Beacon Press, 1960).

The visual mode is a whole body of data that can be used, like language, for composing and understanding messages at many levels of utility from the purely functional to the lofty precincts of artistic expression. It is a body of data composed of constituent parts, a group of units determined by other units, whose significance as a whole is a function of the significance of the parts. How can we define the units and the whole? Through probes, definitions, exercises, observations, and eventually guidelines, which can establish relationships among all the levels of visual expression, all the categories of the visual arts and their "meaning." So often in pursuit of what "art" is, the explorations focus on delineating the role of content in form. In this book the total area of content in form will be investigated at the simplest level: the significance of the individual elements, such as color, tone, line, texture, and proportion; the expressive power of the individual techniques, such as boldness, symmetry, repetition, and accent; and the media context, which serves as the visual setting for design decision, such as painting, photography, architecture, television, and graphics. Inevitably, the final concern of visual literacy is the whole form, the cumulative effect of the combination of selected elements, the manipualtion of the basic units through techniques and their formal compositional relationship to intended meaning.

The cultural and global force of film, photography, and television in the shaping of man's image of himself defines the urgency for teaching visual literacy to both communicators and constituents. In 1935, Moholy-Nagy, the brilliant Bauhaus master, said "the illiterate of the future will be ignorant of pen and camera alike." The future is now. The dramatic potential of universal communication implicit in visual literacy awaits broad, gauged development. In A Primer of Visual Literacy, let us make a modest beginning.

1
THE CHARACTER AND CONTENT OF VISUAL LITERACY

How many see?

What a broad spectrum of processes, activities, functions, attitudes, this simple little question reaches out to encompass. The list is long: to perceive, understand, watch, observe, discover, recognize, visualize, examine, read, look. The connotations are multilateral: from identification of simple objects to the use of symbols and language to conceptualize, from inductive to deductive thinking. The number of questions provoked by just that one question, How many see?, gives a clue to the complexity of the character and content of visual intelligence. That complexity is reflected in the many ways this book will pursue the nature of the visual experience through explorations, analysis, and definition to develop a methodology that makes it possible to educate all people to their maximum ability both as makers and receivers of visual messages, in other words, to make them visually literate.

The first learning experience of a child is through tactile awareness. In addition to this "hands-on" knowledge, recognition includes smelling, hearing, and tasting in a rich contact with the environment. These senses are quickly augmented and superseded by the iconic—the ability to see, to recognize and understand environmental and emotional forces visually. From nearly our first experience of the world, we organize our needs and pleasures, preferences and fears, with great dependence on what we see. Or what we want to see. But this description is only the tip of the iceberg and in no way measures the power and importance the visual sense exerts on our lives. We accept it without realizing that it can be improved just in the basic process of observation or extended into an incomparable tool of human communication. We accept seeing as we experience it—effortlessly.

For the sighted, the process requires little energy; the physiological mechanisms are automatic in the human nervous system. The fact that from this minimal output we receive vast amounts of information in many ways and at many levels provokes little amazement. It all seems natural and simple and suggests that there is no need to do more with our abilities to see and to visualize than just merely to accept them as natural functions. Caleb Gattegno, in his book, To-wards a Visual Culture, comments on the nature of the visual sense: "Sight, even though used by all of us so naturally, has not yet produced its civilization. Sight is swift, comprehensive, simultaneously analytic and synthetic. It requires so little energy to function, as it does, at the speed of light, that it permits our minds to receive and hold an infinite number of items of information in a fraction of a second." Gattegno's observation lays out the startling richness of our visual capability. One is inclined to agree enthusiastically with his conclusions: "With sight infinities are given at once; wealth is its description."

A bias toward visual information is not difficult to find in human behavior. We seek visual reinforcement of our knowledge for many reasons, but primary among them is the directness of the information, the closeness to the real experience. When the American spaceship Apollo 11 landed on the moon, when the first hesitant astronaut's footstep touched the moon's surface, how many among the international television audience that viewed the event would have traded the live transmission of the moment-by-moment action for a detailed, even eloquently written or spoken report of the event? This historic occasion is only one example of the demonstration of the human preference for visual information. There are so many—the snapshot that falls out of the letter from a close friend far away, the three-dimensional model of a new building. Why do we seek visual reinforcement? Seeing is a direct experience and the use of visual data to report information is the closest we can get to the true nature of the reality. The television networks demonstrated their choice. When direct visual connection with the Apollo 11 astronauts was impossible, they broadcast a visual simulation of what was simultaneously being described verbally. Given options, the choice is clear. Not just the astronauts, but also the tourist, the picnic party, the scientist, all turn to the iconic mode, whether to preserve a visual memory or to pursue a technical proof. We all seem to be from Missouri; we all say, "show me."

THE FALSE DICHOTOMY: FINE AND APPLIED ART
Human visual experience is primary in learning to understand and respond to the environment; visual information is the oldest record of human history. The cave paintings represent the oldest preserved report on the world as it was seen some 30,000 years ago. Both facts demonstrate the need to take a new view of the function of not only the process but also the visualizer in society. The greatest stumbling block in this effort is the categorizing of the visual arts into polarities of fine and applied art. At any point in history the definition shifts

and changes, but the most constant factors of differentiation are utility and aesthetics.

Utility describes the design and making of objects and materials and demonstrations that respond to basic needs. From primitive cultures, ancient and contemporary, to today's highly developed technology of manufacture, basic human needs change little. Man needs to eat; to do this, he needs tools to hunt and kill, farm, cut; he needs pots to cook in and utensils from which to eat. He needs to protect his vulnerable body from the changing weather and treacherous environment; for this he needs tools to sew, cut, weave. He needs to stay warm and dry and protected from predatory animals, so he must build some kind of habitat. Subtleties of cultural preference or geographical location exert little pressure on these needs; only interpretation and variation mark the product in terms of creative expression as representative of a particular time or place. In these areas of designing and making the simple necessities of life, it is assumed that every member of the community can not only learn to produce but also can through design and decoration give individual and unique expression to the work. But the self-expression is monitored, first, by the process of learning the craft, and second, by the dictates of functionality. The important factor is that learning how is essential and accepted. The expectation that a member of the community contribute at many levels of visual expression bespeaks a kind of involvement and participation that has withered away in the modern world, and this has been hastened by a number of reasons, but primary among them is the contemporary concept of "fine" art.

The most frequently cited difference between the utilitarian and the purely artistic is the measure of motivation toward producing the beautiful. This is the realm of aesthetics, the inquiry into the nature of sense perception, the experience of beauty, possibly just artistic beauty. But the purposes of the visual arts are many. Socrates raises the question "of whether aesthetic experiences have intrinsic worth or are to be valued or deprecated by their stimulation of the profitable and good." "Experience of beauty affords no kind of knowledge, historical, scientific, or philosophical," says Immanuel Kant. "It can be called true because it makes us more aware of our mental activity." However they approach the problem, the philosophers agree that art has subject matter, emotions, passions, feelings. In the wide range of the various visual arts, religious, social, or domestic, the subject matter changes with the intent, having in common only the ability to communicate specifically or in the abstract. As Henri Bergson puts it, "Art is only a more direct vision of reality." In other words, even at this lofty level of evaluation, the visual arts have some function or utility. It is easy to draw a diagram to place various of the visual formats in some relationship to these polarities. Figure 1.1 presents one way of expressing contemporary evaluative attitudes.

FINE ART   PAINTING   SCULPTURE   MONUMENTS   ARCHITECTURE   CRAFTS   ILLUSTRATION   PHOTOGRAPHY   GRAPHICS   INDUSTRIAL DESIGN   APPLIED ART

FIGURE 1.1

Such a diagram would look quite different were it to represent another culture, such as the Pre-Renaissance (1.2),

FINE ART   ARCHITECTURE   SCULPTURE   PAINTING   CRAFTS   APPLIED ART

FIGURE 1.2

or the "Bauhaus" point of view, which would group any and all of the fine and applied arts on one central point in the continuum (1.3).

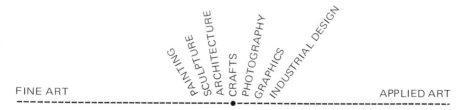

FINE ART   PAINTING SCULPTURE ARCHITECTURE CRAFTS PHOTOGRAPHY GRAPHICS INDUSTRIAL DESIGN   APPLIED ART

FIGURE 1.3

Long before the Bauhaus, William Morris and the Pre-Raphaelites had inclinations in the same direction. "Art," said Ruskin, who was their spokesman, "is all one, any distinction between fine and applied art is destructive and artificial." The Pre-Raphaelites added one distinction to their thesis that put them totally out of sympathy with the later philosophy of the Bauhaus—they rejected all work of the machine. What is made by hand is beautiful, they believed, and though they espoused a cause of sharing art with all, turning their backs on the possibilities of mass production was an obvious negation of their self-proclaimed purposes.

What the Morris-led "Arts and Crafts" group did recognize in their reaching back to the past to renew interest in careful and proud workmanship was the impossibility of producing art without craftsmanship—a fact easily forgotten in the snobbish dichotomy between fine and applied in the arts. During the Renaissance, the artist learned his craft from the simple tasks on, and despite his high estate, shared his guild or union with the basic craftsman. This provided for a stronger apprentice system, and, more important, less specialization. There was a free flow back and forth between the artist and craftsman, each able to participate in all levels of work, barred only by a measure of competence. But, as times change, modes change. What is labeled "art" can change as fast as the people who label it. "A hallelujah chorus," says Carl Sandburg, in his poem, "The People, Yes," "forever shifting its star soloist."

The contemporary view of the visual arts moves beyond the polarities of "fine" and "applied" art to questions of subjective expression and objective function and again has tended toward the association of individual interpretation with creative expression belonging to the "fine arts" and the response to purpose and use belonging to the "applied arts." An easel painter working for himself without commission pleases himself first without thought of the market place, and is, therefore, almost totally subjective. A craftsman fashioning a clay pot can appear to be equally subjective. He is making his pot in a shape and size to please his own taste. He has, however, a practical concern: can the design that pleases him also hold water? This modification of utility imposes on a designer some measure of objectivity not so immediately necessary or so apparent in the work of the easel painter. The American architect Sullivan's dictum, "form follows function," is most dynamically illustrated by the airplane designer, whose own preferences are limited by what assembled shapes, proportions, and materials will, in fact, really fly. The final product is shaped by what it does. But in the subtler problems of design, there are many products that can reflect the subjective tastes of the designer and still function perfectly well. It is not only the designer that must face problems of compromise in the matters of personal taste. Frequently an artist or a sculptor must modify a work because he has received his commission from a patron who knows exactly what he wants. Michelangelo's long wrangles about his commissions from two Popes are the liveliest and most descriptive examples of the problem an artist has in controlling his subjective notions in order to please a patron. And yet, no one would consider "The Last Judgment" or "David" commercial works.

Michelangelo's fresco for the ceiling of the Sistine Chapel aptly demonstrates the weakness of this false dichotomy. The Pope, as the representative of the needs of the Church, influenced Michelangelo's own ideas which were also modified by the direct purpose of the mural. It was a visual explanation of the "Creation" to an audience, largely illiterate, and therefore unable to read the Biblical story, or if they could read, unable to imagine in such palpable fashion the story's drama. The mural is a balance between the subjective and the objective approach of the artist, and a comparable balance between pure artistic expression and utility of purpose. This delicate balance is extraordinarily rare in the visual arts, but when it is struck, it has the exactness of a bull's-eye. Who would question this mural as authentic "fine art," and yet it has a purpose and utility that contradict the definition of the so-called difference between fine and applied art: "applied" art should be functional and "fine" art without utility. This snobbish attitude influences many artists on both sides of the fence and creates an atmosphere of alienation and confusion. Oddly enough, it is a fairly recent development. The idea of a "work of art" is a modern one, reinforced by the concept of the museum as the ultimate repository of the beautiful. A public, enthusiastically interested in worshipping at the altar of beauty in a museum, approaches it unmoved by an incredibly ugly environment. This attitude removes art from the mainstream, gives it an aura of being special and petty, reserves it for an elite, and so negates the true fact of how it is struck through our lives and our world. If we accept this point of view, we abdicate a valuable part of our human potential. We not only become consumers with not very sharp criteria, but we deny the essential importance of visual communication both historically and in our own lives.

THE IMPACT OF THE PHOTOGRAPH
The last bastion of exclusiveness of the "artist" is that one special

talent, the ability to draw, to replicate the environment as it appears. The camera, in all its forms, has ended that. It forms the final connecting link between the innate ability to see and the external capability to report, interpret, express what we see, without having to have special talent or extended training to effect the process. There is little doubt that contemporary life style has been influenced, and crucially, by the changes enacted on it by the fact of the photograph. In print, language is the primary element, while visual factors, such as the physical setting or design format and illustration, are secondary or supportive. In the modern media, just the reverse is true. The visual dominates; the verbal augments. Print is not dead yet, nor will it ever be, but, nevertheless, our language-dominated culture has moved perceptibly toward the iconic. Most of what we know and learn, what we buy and believe, what we recognize and desire, is determined by the domination of the human psyche by the photograph. And it will be more so in the future.

The measure of the influence of the photograph in all its many variations and permutations is a throwback to the importance in life of our eyes. Arthur Koestler, in his book, The Act of Creation, observes: "Thinking in pictures dominates the manifestations of the unconscious, the dream, the hypnogogic half dream, the psychotic's hallucinations, the artist's vision. (The visionary prophet seems to have been a visualizer, and not a verbalizer; the highest compliment we pay to those who trade in verbal currency is to call them 'visionary thinkers')." When we see, we do so many things: we experience what is happening in a direct way; we discover something we never noticed or possibly never even looked for before; we become aware through a series of visual experiences of something we eventually come to recognize and know; we watch for evolving changes through patient observation. Both the word and the process of seeing have come to have much broader implications. To see has come to mean understanding. The man from Missouri who is shown something presumably has a deeper understanding than someone who is told about it.

Here the implications are most important for visual literacy. To expand our ability to see means to expand our ability to understand a visual message and, even more crucial, to make a visual message. Vision involves more than just seeing or being shown. It is an integral part of the communication process which encompasses all considerations of fine art, applied art, subjective expression, response to functional purpose.

VISUAL KNOWLEDGE AND VERBAL LANGUAGE

Visualizing is the ability to form mental pictures. We remember a way through city streets to a destination, maneuvering in our mind over a route from one place to another, checking visual clues, rejecting, doubling back, and we do all this before we proceed with the journey. All in our minds. But even more mysterious and magical, we form the sight of something we never saw before. Vision, previsualization, is intricately linked to the creative leap, the Eureka syndrome, as a primary means of problem solving. And it is this very process of moving around in mental images in imagination that frequently takes us to the point of breakthrough and solution. Koestler, again, in The Act of Creation, sees it this way: "Thinking in concepts emerged from thinking in images through the slow development of the powers of abstraction and symbolization, just as the phonetic script emerged by similar processes out of pictorial symbols and hieroglyphics." A great lesson in communication can be learned from this progression. The evolution of language started with pictures, progressed to pictographs, self-explaining cartoons, to phonetic units, and then to the alphabet, which R. L. Gregory in The Intelligent Eye so aptly calls, "the mathematic of meaning." Each step of the way was, no doubt, a progression toward more efficient communication. But, there are many indications that there is a retracing of this process back to the picture, again inspired by the seeking of more efficiency. The most important question is literacy and what it means in the context of language and what analogies can be drawn from language and applied to visual information.

Language has held a unique place in human learning. It has functioned as a means of storing and transporting information, a vehicle for exchanging ideas, and as a way for the human mind to conceptualize. Logos, the Greek word for language, also carries collateral meaning of thought and reason in the English word derived from it, logic. The implications are quite obvious; language is seen as a means for a higher form of thinking than the visual and tactile modes. But the assumption is subject to some question and investigation. To begin with, language and verbal literacy are not the same thing. Being able to speak a language is vastly different from achieving literacy through reading and writing, even though we can learn to understand and use language at both operative levels. But only spoken language evolves naturally. Noam Chomsky's work in linguistics indicates that the deep structure of language is biologically innate. Verbal literacy, reading and writing, must, however, be learned through a number of steps. First, we learn a symbol system, abstract shapes that represent designated sounds. These symbols are our ABC, the alpha and beta of the Greek language from which we have named the whole group of sound-symbols or letters, the alphabet. We learn our alphabet as individual letters, and then we learn the combinations of letters and their sounds which we call words, the stand-ins or surrogates for things and ideas and actions. Knowing the meaning of words is knowing the common definitions they share. The final step in achieving verbal literacy involves learning the common syntax to establish limits of construction according to accepted usage. These are the rudiments, the irreducibly basic elements of language. When they are mastered, it is possible to read and write, to express and understand written information. This is a most cursory description. But, it is apparent that even in its most simplified state, verbal literacy represents a structure with technical plans and agreed-on definitions, which, by comparison, characterize visual communication as almost totally lacking in organization. So it would appear.

VISUAL LITERACY
The major pitfall in developing an approach to visual literacy is trying to overdefine it. The existence of language, a communication mode of comparatively neatly organized structure, no doubt exerts strong pressure on all those who pursue the very idea of visual literacy. If one means of communication is so easy to break down into component parts and structure, why not the other? Any symbol system is an invention of man. The symbol systems we call language are inventions or refinements of what was once the object perceptions in picture-strip mentality. Hence there are many symbol systems and many languages, some related by their derivations from the same root, some totally unrelated. Numbers, for instance, are surrogates for a unique information retrieval system, as also are notes in music. In each case, the ease of learning the encoded information is based on the original synthesis of the system. The meanings are attached and each system has syntactical ground rules. There are more than 3,000 languages, separate and unique, in current usage in the world, each different. The language of vision is, by comparison, so much more universal that its complexity should not be regarded as too difficult to be worthwhile overcoming. Languages are logical wholes. But no such simplicity can be ascribed to visual intelligence, and those of us who have labored to make it analogous to language have been engaged in an exercise in futility.

But the use of the word "literacy" in conjunction with the word "visual" does have enormous significance. Sight is natural; making and understanding visual messages is natural to a point, but effectiveness on either level can only be achieved through study. In pursuit of visual literacy, one problem must be clearly identified and avoided. In verbal literacy, long before words such as "creative" are applied as a value judgment, it is expected of educated people that they be capable of reading and writing. The writing does not necessarily have to be brilliant; clear, understandable prose, correctly spelled and syntactically sound, will do. Verbal literacy can be achieved at quite a simple level of making and understanding written messages. It can be characterized as a tool. Being able to read and write, by the very nature of its function, does not demand by implication the need for higher expression, the production of novels or poetry. We accept the idea of verbal literacy as operative at many levels, from simple messages to increasingly complex and artistic forms.

Partly because of the separation in the visual of art and craft, and partly because of the limitations in the talent for drawing, much of visual communication has been left to intuition and happenstance. Since no attempt to analyze or define it has been made in terms of the structure of the visual mode, no method of application can be attained. Indeed, the educational system is moving with monolithic slowness in this area, still persisting in an emphasis on the verbal mode to the exclusion of the rest of the human sensorium and with little sensitivity, if any, to the overwhelmingly visual character of the child's learning experience. Even the use of a visual approach to learning through the media is without rigor and purpose. In many instances, students are bombarded with visual aids—film loops, films, slides, slide sound presentations—but the presentation reinforces their passive experience as consumers of television. Media materials being produced and used for educational purposes are presented with few criteria for evaluating and understanding the effects they produce. The consumer of most of the educational media production would not, to make the verbal literacy analogy, recognize or know what was a misspelling, an incorrectly phrased sentence, a badly organized theme. The same is so often true in the "hands on" media experience. The only guidelines for the use of cameras in making intelligent messages are drawn from literary traditions rather than from the structure and integrity of the visual mode itself. One of the tragedies of the overwhelming potential of visual literacy at all levels of education is the mindless, custodial-playtime function the visual arts serve in the curriculum and the similar state that exists in the use of media, cameras, film, television. Why, in the visual arts, all of them, have we fallen heir to an unspoken devotion to nonintellectualism? Examination of the education system reveals that the development of constructive methods of visual learning are ignored except for those students who are especially interested and gifted. Judgments of what is workable, appropriate, effective in visual communication have been abandoned to whim, some formless definition of taste, or to the subjective, self-reflexive evaluation of the sender or receiver with little or no attempt to realize, at the least, some of the prescribed levels we expect of what we call literacy in the verbal mode. This is probably not so much from bias as from a firm conviction that no methodology, no means for achieving visual literacy, is possible. However, the demand for media study has outstripped the capabilities of our schools and colleges. Facing the challenge of visual literacy may no longer be so easy to ignore.

How have we arrived at this stalemate? Of all the means of human communication, the visual alone has no regimen, no methodology, no single system with prescribed guidelines for either expression or understanding of visual methods. Why, when we want it and need it so much, does visual literacy elude us? Obviously, a new approach must be evolved to solve this dilemma.

AN APPROACH TO VISUAL LITERACY
We know so much of the human sensorium, particularly of sight. Not everything, but a great deal. We also have many working systems for the study and analysis of the components of visual messages. Unfortunately, all this has not been put together in a viable form. By categorizing and analyzing, we may, indeed, be revealing what has always been there, the beginnings of a workable approach to universal visual literacy.

We must search for visual literacy in many places and many ways, in the methods for training artists, in the technical training of craftsmen and artisans, in psychological theory, in nature, and in the physiological workings of the human organism itself.

There is visual syntax. There are guidelines for constructing compositions. There are basic elements that can be learned and understood by all students of the visual media, artists and nonartists alike, and that, along with manipulative techniques, can be used to create clear visual messages. Knowledge of all these factors can lead to clearer comprehension of visual messages.

We understand visual information in many ways. Perception and kin-esthetic forces, physiological in character, are vital to the visual process. How we stand, move, keep our balance, protect ourselves; the way we react to light and dark or to sudden movement are factors in how we receive and interpret visual messages. All of these responses are natural and operate without effort; we do not have to study them or learn how to do them. But, they are influenced and possibly modified by psychological moods and cultural conditioning and lastly, by environmental expectation. How we view the world frequently affects what we see. The process is, after all, a very individual one for each of us. The control of the psyche is very often programmed by social mores. Just as some cultural groups eat things others would be sickened by, we have visual preferences ingrained in us. The individual who grows up in the modern Western world is conditioned to the techniques of perspective which present a synthetic, three-dimensional world through both painting and photography, media that are, in fact, flat and two-dimensional. An aborigine has to learn to decode the synthetic representation of dimension through perspective in a photograph. He has to learn the convention; he cannot see it naturally. Environment also has profound control on how we see. The mountain dweller, for instance, has to reorient his way of seeing on a flat, endless plain. Nowhere is this more evident than in the art of the Eskimo. Having experienced so much undifferentiated white snow and light sky in the environment, which results in obscuring the reference of the horizon, the Eskimo artist takes liberties with right side up and upside down.

Despite these modifications, there is a basic, perceptual visual system, one that all human beings have in common; but the system is subject to variations, variations on basic structural themes. There is visual syntax and its dominant characteristic is complexity. The complexity, however, does not defy definition.

One thing is certain. Visual literacy cannot ever be a clear-cut logical system similar to language. Languages are made-up systems constructed by man to encode, store, and decode information. Therefore, their structure has a logic that visual literacy is unable to parallel.

SOME CHARACTERISTICS OF VISUAL MESSAGES
The inclination toward wanting to connect the verbal and visual structure is totally understandable. One of the reasons is natural. Visual

data has three distinctive and individual levels: the visual input, which consists of myriad symbol systems; the representational visual material we recognize in the environment and can replicate in drawing, painting, sculpture, and film; and the abstract understructure, the form of everything we see, whether natural or composed for intended effects.

There is a vast world of symbols that identify actions or organizations, moods, directions—symbols ranging from those rich in representational detail to those that are completely abstract and so unrelated to recognizable information that they must be learned the same way we learn language. Man has gone through the slow and difficult steps of putting down in preservable form the familiar events and gestures of his experience, and from this process written language has evolved. At first, words are represented by pictures and where that is not feasible, a symbol is invented. Eventually, in highly developed written language, pictures are abandoned and sounds are represented by symbols. Unlike the pictures, the symbols require few special skills to reproduce. Literacy is infinitely more possible for the majority with the sound symbol language, because it is so simplified. English employs only 26 symbols in its alphabet. However, languages that never get beyond the pictograph stage, like Chinese, where the picture-word symbols, or ideograms, number in the thousands, hold grave problems for mass literacy. The Chinese call writing and the drawing of pictures by the same name, calligraphy. This indicates some special visual skills are needed to write Chinese. But pictographs are not pictures. R. L. Gregory in The Intelligent Eye calls them, "cartoons of cartoons."

But even where they exist as a major component of the visual mode, symbols function differently than language and, in fact, understandable and even tempting though it may be, the attempt to find guidelines for visual literacy in the structure of language simply won't work. But as a force in visual literacy, symbols have enormous importance and viability.

The same usefulness for composing visual materials and messages lies in the other two levels of visual intelligence. Knowing how they function in the process of seeing and how they are understood can contribute enormously to the understanding of their application to communication.

The representational level of visual intelligence is governed strongly
by direct experience which extends beyond perception. We learn
about things we are prevented from experiencing directly through visual media, through demonstrations, through examples in model form.
Although a verbal description can be an extremely effective explanation, the visual means are quite different in character from language,
particularly in their directness. No intervening coded systems need 'be
employed to facilitate understanding, no decoding to delay comprehension. Seeing a process is sometimes enough to be able to understand how it functions. Seeing an object sometimes provides enough
knowledge to evaluate and understand it. This fact of observation
serves not only as an enabling device for learning but also as our closest link to the reality of our surroundings. We trust our eyes and we
depend on them.

The last level of visual intelligence is possibly the most difficult to describe and may in the end be the most crucial to the development
of visual literacy. It is the understructure, the abstract elemental composition and, therefore, the pure visual message. Anton Ehrenzweig
has developed a theory of art based on a primary process of development and viewing, namely the conscious level, and a secondary level,
the preconscious. He elaborates on this classification of the structural
levels of the visual mode by associating Piaget's term, "syncretistic,"
for the child's vision of the world through his art with the concept of
undifferentiation. Ehrenzweig describes the child as able to see the
entire whole in a "global" vision. This talent, he believes, is never de-
stroyed in the adult and can be employed as "a potent tool." Another way of analyzing this duplex system of seeing is to recognize that
everything we see and design is composed of the basic visual elements,
the skeletal visual force, crucial to meaning and powerful to response.
It is inextricably part of all we see, whatever its nature, realistic or abstract. It is the pure, stripped-down visual energy.

A number of disciplines have tackled the problem of finding where
meaning comes from in the visual arts. Artists, art historians, philosophers, and specialists from various fields of the humanities and social
sciences have a long history of exploring how and what it is that the
visual arts "communicate." I believe some of the most meaningful
work has been done by "Gestalt" psychologists, whose major interest
has been in the principles of perceptual organization, the process of
making wholes out of parts. The underlying point of view of Gestalt,
as defined by von Ehrenfels, pointed out that "if each of twelve ob-

servers listened to one of the twelve tones of a melody, the sum of
their experience would not correspond to what would be perceived
if someone listened to the whole melody." Rudolf Arnheim has
done brilliant work in applying much of the Gestalt theory developed
by Wertheimer, Köhler, and Koffka to the interpretation of the visual arts. He explores not only the workings of perception but also the
quality of the individual visual units and the strategies of their unifi-
cation into a final and complete whole. In all visual stimuli, on all
levels of visual intelligence, meaning may lie not only in the representational data, the environmental information, in the symbols including
language, but also in the compositional forces that exist or coexist
with the factual, visual statement. Any visual event is a form with
content, but the content is highly influenced by the significance of
the constituent parts, such as color, tone, texture, dimension, proportion, and their compositional relationships to meaning. In Symbols
and Civilization, Ralph Ross talks only of "art" when he observes
that it "yields an experience of the kind we call aesthetic, an experience most of us have in the presence of beauty, which gives deep satisfactions. Exactly why we have these satisfactions has puzzled philosophers for centuries, but it seems clear that they depend somehow
on the qualities and organization of a work of art including its meanings, not on meanings in isolation." Words like meaning, experience,
aesthetic, beauty, all overlap at the same point of interest, namely,
what it is we get out of the visual experience and how. This encompasses the entire visual experience at every level in every way.

To begin to answer these questions the individual components of the
visual process must be examined in the most simplified form. The
tool box of all visual communications is the basic elements, the compositional source, for all kinds of visual materials and messages and
objects and experiences: the dot, the minimal visual unit, pointer,
marker of space; the line, the fluid, restless articulator of form, in the
probing looseness of the sketch and the tighter technical plan; shape,
the basic shapes, circle, square, triangle, and all their endless variations, combinations, permutations, planal and dimensional; direction,
the thrust of movement that incorporates and reflects the character
of the basic shapes, circular, diagonal, perpendicular; tone, the presence or absence of light, by which we see; color, the coordinate of
tone with the added component of chroma, the most emotional and
expressive visual element; texture, optical or tactile, the surface character of visual materials; scale or proportion, the relative size and
measurement; dimension and motion, both as frequently implied as

expressed. These are the visual elements; from them we draw the raw material of all levels of visual intelligence and from them all varieties of visual statements and objects and environments and experiences are planned and expressed.

The visual elements are manipulated with shifting emphasis by the techniques of visual communication in direct response to the character of what is being designed and the message purpose. The most dynamic of the visual techniques is contrast, which exists on a polarity with its opposite technique of harmony. The use of techniques does not have to be thought of as only operative in extremes, but can be expanded into subtle steps on a continuum from one polarity to the other, like the steps of gray between black and white. There are many techniques that can be applied in the search for visual solutions. Here are some of the most often used and easily identified techniques, arranged to demonstrate their opposite source:

Contrast	Harmony
Instability	Balance
Asymmetry	Symmetry
Irregularity	Regularity
Complexity	Simplicity
Fragmentation	Unity
Intricacy	Economy
Exaggeration	Understatement
Spontaneity	Predictability
Activeness	Stasis
Boldness	Subtlety
Accent	Neutrality
Transparency	Opacity
Variation	Consistency
Distortion	Accuracy
Depth	Flatness
Juxtaposition	Singularity
Randomness	Sequentiality
Sharpness	Diffusion
Episodicity	Repetition

The techniques are the agents in the visual communication process; it is through their energy that the character of a visual solution takes form. The options are vast and the formats and media many; the three levels of the visual structure interact. However overwhelming the numbers of choices that are open to the visual problem solver, it is the techniques that will serve most effectively as connectors between intention and result. Conversely, a familiarity with the nature of techniques will make a more discerning audience for any visual statement.

In the pursuit of visual literacy we must concern ourselves with each of the above areas of analysis and definition; the structural forces that exist in the interactive relationship between the visual stimuli and the human organism functionally, both physically and psychologically; the character of the visual elements; and the forming power of the techniques. In addition, visual solutions should be governed by intended meaning and posture through style, personal and cultural. And the last consideration is the medium itself, which through its own character and limitations will legislate the methods of solution. At each step of the explorations, exercises will be suggested for expanding the understanding of the nature of visual expression.

In all its many aspects the process is complex. Nevertheless, complexity need not be a hindrance in understanding the visual mode. True, it is easier to have one set of common definitions and limits for construction or composition, but simplicity has negative aspects. The simpler the formula, the more limited the potential for creative variation and expression. Far from being negative, the three-leveled functionality of visual intelligence—realistic, abstract, symbolic—offers harmonious interaction, syncretistic though it may be.

When we see, we are doing many things at once. We are seeing an enormous field peripherally. We are seeing in an up-to-down, left-to-right movement. We are imposing on what we are isolating in our field of vision not only implied axes to adjust balance but also a structural map to chart and measure the action of the compositional forces that are so vital to content and, therefore, to message input and output. All of this is happening while at the same time we are decoding all manner of symbols.

It is a multidimensional process, whose most striking characteristic is its simultaneity. And each function is linked to process, to circumstance. For not only does sight offer us method options for information retrieval, but options that coexist and are available and operative at the same moment. The results are astonishing, no matter how conditioned we may be to take them for granted. With the speed of light, visual intelligence delivers multiple bits of information, simultaneously serving as a dynamic channel for communication and a still hardly recognized aid to education. Is this the reason the visually active seem to learn better? Gattegno has put it masterfully in <u>Towards a Visual Culture</u>: "Man has functioned as a seer and embraced vastness for millennia. But only recently, through television (and film and photography, the modern media) has he been able to shift from the clumsiness of speech (however miraculous and far-reaching) as a means of expression and therefore of communication, to the powers of infinite visual expression, thus enabling him to share with everybody immense dynamic wholes in no time."

There is no easy way to develop visual literacy, but it is as vital to our teaching of the modern media as reading and writing was to print. It may, indeed, be the crucial component of all channels of communication now and in the future. As long as information was primarily stored and distributed in language and the artist was regarded by society as alone in his unique ability to communicate visually, universal verbal literacy was considered essential, but visual intelligence was largely ignored. The invention of the camera has brought about a dramatic new view of communication and, collaterally, of education. The camera, the cinema, television, EVR video cartridges, and video tape, and visual media not yet in currency will modify our definition—not only of education but also of intelligence itself. First, a re-examination of our basic visual abilities is in order. Second, a need to pursue and develop a structural system and a methodology for teaching and learning how to express and interpret ideas visually is urgent. An area that was once the exclusive province of the artist and designer - must now be considered the concern of both those who work in any of the visual media and their audience.

If art is, as Bergson defined it, a "direct vision of reality," then surely the modern media can be considered quite seriously as natural means for artistic expression, since they present and replicate life almost as in a mirror. "Oh wad some power the giftie gie us," pleads Robert Burns, "to see oursels as others see us." And the media respond with their vast powers. But, not only have the media made available their magic to audiences, they have placed their magic firmly in the hands of anyone who wishes to use the media for expression of ideas.

In a never-ending evolution of technical equipment, photography and film are constantly simplified to be used for many purposes. But the technical prowess in handling equipment is not enough. The character of the media accentuates the need for understanding their visual components. An intellectual, trained ability to make and understand visual messages is becoming a vital necessity to involvement with communication. It is quite likely that visual literacy will be one of the fundamental measures of education in the last third of our century.

Art and the meaning of art has changed sharply in the technological age, but the aesthetic of art has not responded to the change. The opposite has happened: as the character of the visual arts and their relationship to society has shifted dramatically, the aesthetic of art has become more fixed. The result is a diffused notion that the visual arts are solely the province of subjective intuition, as shallow a judgment as the overemphasis of literal meaning would be. In fact, visual expression is the product of highly complex intelligence, of which we have pitifully little understanding. What you see is a major part of what you know, and visual literacy can help us to see what we see and know what we know.

EXERCISES

1. Choose an example from either your own possessions or from a magazine photograph of an object that has value in terms of both fine and applied art. Make a list evaluating its functionality, its aesthetic beauty, its communication (what it does to expand your knowledge of yourself, your environment, world, past, future), and its decorative or entertainment value.

2. Cut a photograph out of a magazine or newspaper and write a list of one-word or short-phrased responses you have to it in terms of its literal message as well as its underlying compositional meaning and include the response to any symbols (language or other symbols) that are included in it. After you have analyzed the photograph, write a paragraph that completely reports what the photograph does and which could be used as a replacement for it.

3. Choose a snapshot you have taken or anything you have designed or made (drawing, embroidery, garden, living arrangement, clothes) and analyze what effect or message you intended. Ask someone what message or effect you have created. Compare the intentions with the responses.

2

COMPOSITION:
THE SYNTACTICAL GUIDELINES FOR VISUAL LITERACY

The process of composition is the most crucial step in visual problem
solving. The results of the compositional decisions set the purpose
and meaning of the visual statement and carry strong implications for
what the viewer receives. It is at this vital stage in the creative process
that the visual communicator has the strongest control of the work
and the greatest opportunity to express the total mood the work is
intended to convey. But the visual mode offers no proscribed structural systems that are absolute. How can we gain control of our complex visual means with some certainty of shared meaning in the final
results? In language syntax means the orderly arrangement of words
in their appropriate form and order. The rules are defined: all one has
to do is learn them and use them intelligently. But syntax in the context of visual literacy can only mean the orderly arrangement of
parts, leaving us with the problem of how we can approach the process of composition with intelligence and knowledge of how compositional decisions will affect the final result. There are no absolute
rules, but there is a great deal of understanding of what will occur in
terms of meaning if we make certain arrangements of the parts
toward organizing and orchestrating the visual means. Many of the
guidelines for understanding the meaning in visual form, the syntactical potential of structure in visual literacy, stem from the investigation of the process of human perception.

PERCEPTION AND VISUAL COMMUNICATION
Meaning in visual message-making lies not only in the cumulative effects of the arrangement of the basic elements but also in the perceptual mechanism that is universally shared by the human organism.
More simply put: we create a design out of many colors and shapes
and textures and tones and relative proportions; we relate these elements interactively; we intend meaning. The result is the composition,
the artist's or photographer's or designer's intention. It is his input.
Seeing is another and separate step in visual communication. It is the
process of absorbing information into the nervous system through the
eyes, the sense of sight. This process and capacity is shared by all people on a more or less common basis, finding its significance in terms
of shared meaning. The two separate steps, seeing and designing and/
or making are interdependent for both meaning in a general sense and
message in the case of attempting to respond to a specific communication. Between the general meaning, mood, or ambience of visual infor-

mation and a specific, defined message lies yet another area of visual meaning, functionality, in the objects that are designed, made, and manufactured to serve a purpose. While it would seem that the message of such works is secondary to their viability, the facts prove otherwise. Clothes, houses, public buildings, even the whittling and scrimshaw of amateur craftsmen tell us an enormous amount about the people who designed and chose them. And our understanding of a culture depends on our study of the world they built and the tools and artifacts and art they created.

Primarily, the act of seeing involves a response to light. In other words, the most important and necessary element in the visual experience is tonal. All of the other visual elements are revealed to us through light, but they are secondary to the element of tone, which is, in fact, light or the absence of light. What light reveals and offers us is the substance by which man fashions and devises what he recognizes and identifies in the environment, namely all the other visual elements: line, color, shape, direction, texture, scale, dimension, motion. Which elements dominate which visual statements is determined by the nature of what is being designed or, in the case of nature, what exists. But when we define painting elementally as tonal, filled with shape reference and consequently direction, having texture and tone-color, possibly scale reference and no dimension and motion except by implication, it does not even begin to define the visual potential of painting. The possible variations of a visual statement that fits neatly within that description is literally infinite. Those variations depend on the artist's subjective expression through emphasis of certain elements over others and the manipulation of those elements through the strategic choice of techniques. In these choices, the artist finds his meaning.

The final result is the artist's true statement. But meaning also depends on the response of the viewer, who also modifies and interprets through the net of subjective judgment. One factor alone is common currency between artist and audience, in fact, among all people—the physical system of their visual perceptions, the psychophysiological components of the nervous system, the mechanical workings, the sensory apparatus through which they see.

Gestalt psychology has contributed valuable research and experimentation in the area of perception, collecting data and searching the significance of visual patterns, as well as finding how the human organ-

ism sees and organizes visual input and articulates visual output. Together, the physical and the psychological are relative and not absolute. Every visual pattern has a dynamic quality that cannot be defined intellectually, emotionally, or mechanically by size or direction
or shape or distance. These stimuli are only the static measurements,
but the psychophysical forces they set off, like those of any stimuli,
modify space and arrange or derange balance. Together they create
the perception of a design or an environment or a thing. All things
visual are not just something that happens out there. They are visual
events, total occurrences, actions that incorporate the reaction into
the whole.

Abstract as the psychophysiological elements of visual syntax may be,
they can be defined as to their general character. The meaning inherent in abstract expression is intense; it short-circuits the intellect,
making contact directly with the emotions and feelings, encapsulat-
ing the essential meaning, cutting through the conscious to the unconscious.

Visual information may also have definable form either through attached meaning in symbols or through shared experience in the environment, in life. Up, down, blue sky, vertical trees, scratchy sand,
red-orange-yellow fire, are but a few of the denotative, point-at-able
qualities we all share visually. And so, whether consciously or not,
we respond with some conformity to their meaning.

BALANCE
The most important psychological as well as physical influence on
human perception is man's need for balance, to have his two feet
planted firmly on the ground and to know if he is to remain upright
in any circumstance, in any attitude, with some reasonable certainty.
Equilibrium, then, is man's firmest and strongest visual reference,
both his conscious and unconscious basis for making visual judgments.
The extraordinary fact is that while all visual patterns have a center
of gravity which can be technically computed, no method of calcula-
tion is as fast, as accurate, as automatic as the intuitive sense of balance inherent in man's perceptions.

So the horizontal-vertical construct is the basic relationship of man
to his environment. But beyond the simple, static balance shown in
Figure 2.1 is the process of adjustment to each variation of weight
through a response of counterpoise (2.2 and 2.3). This internalized
awareness of steady uprightness in relationship to a stable base is ex-

FIGURE 2.1   FIGURE 2.2   FIGURE 2.3

pressed externally through the visual establishment of Figure 2.4 and
a horizontal-vertical relationship of what is being viewed (2.5) and its
relative weight in relationship to a balanced state (2.6). Balance is as
fundamental in nature as it is in man. It is the state opposite to collapse. You can measure the effect of disequilibrium by observing the
look of alarm on the face of a victim who has suddenly and without
warning been pushed off balance.

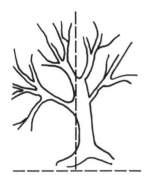

FIGURE 2.4   FIGURE 2.5   FIGURE 2.6

In visual expression or interpretation, this process of stabilization imposes on all things seen and planned a vertical "axis" with a horizontal secondary referrent which together establish the structural factors
that measure balance. This visual axis is also called a felt axis which
better expresses the unseen but dominating presence of the axis in
the act of seeing. It is an unconscious constant.

STRESS

Many things in the environment appear to have no stability. A circle
is a good example. It seems the same however we look at it (2.7), but

in the act of seeing, we supply it with stability by imposing on it the vertical axis that analyzes and determines its balance as a form (2.8) and then (2.9) adding the horizontal base as a reference that completes the sense of stability. Projecting the hidden (or felt) structural

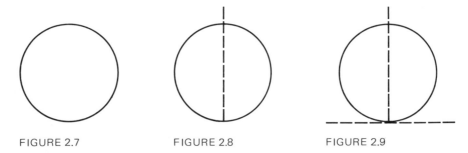

FIGURE 2.7   FIGURE 2.8   FIGURE 2.9

factors onto regular forms, such as a circle, or square, or an equilateral triangle, is comparatively simple and easy to understand, but when a form is irregular, the analysis and establishment of balance is more involved and intricate (see Figure 2.10). This stabilization process can be demonstrated with greater clarity through a sequence of slight changes in the examples and the responses of the position of the felt axis to the shifting state of balance in Figure 2.11.

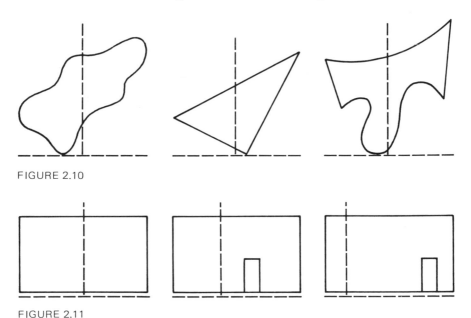

FIGURE 2.10

FIGURE 2.11

This process of ordering, of intuitively recognizing regularity or the lack of it, is an unconscious one, requiring no explanation or verbalization. For both the sender and the receiver of visual information the lack of balance and regularity is a disorienting factor. In other words, it is the most effective of all visual means in creating an effect in response to message purpose, an effect that has a direct and economic potential for conveying visual information. The visual options are polarities, either regularity and simplicity (2.12) on the one hand, or complex and unexpected variation (2.13) on the other. Choice between these options governs relative response from the viewer with either repose and relaxation or stress.

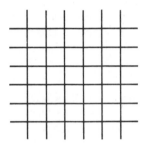
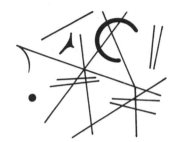

FIGURE 2.12. REPOSE   FIGURE 2.13. STRESS

The connection between relative stress and relative balance can be demonstrated simply in any regular form. For example, a tipped radius in a circle (2.14) exerts greater visual stress because the radius does not confrom to the unseen "visual axis" and therefore unsettles the balance. The visible element, the radius, is modified by the invisible element, the felt axis (2.15), as well as by its relationship to the horizontal, stabilizing base (2.16). In terms of design, plan, purpose: of two circles side by side, it is the one with the tipped or nonconforming radius (2.18 rather than 2.17) which attracts the attention of the viewer most.

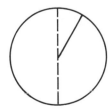
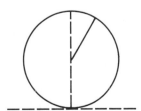

FIGURE 2.14   FIGURE 2.15   FIGURE 2.16

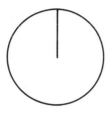 

FIGURE 2.17   FIGURE 2.18

There is no judgment to attach to this phenomenon of stress. It is neither good or bad. Its value in the theory of perception lies in how it is used in visual communication, that is, how it can reinforce meaning, purpose, intention and, further, how it can be used as a basis for interpretation and understanding. Stress, or its absence, is the first compositional factor that can be used syntactically in the pursuit of visual literacy.

There are many aspects of stress that should be expanded on, but, first, consider that stress (the unexpected, the most irregular, complex, unstable) does not alone dominate the eye. There are other factors in the sequence of seeing which contribute to attention-getting and compositional dominance. The process of establishing the vertical axis and horizontal base draws the eye with much more intensity to both visual areas, automatically giving them relative importance compositionally. As already demonstrated, it is easy to locate these areas in regular shapes, shown in Figure 2.19. In more complex shapes, the

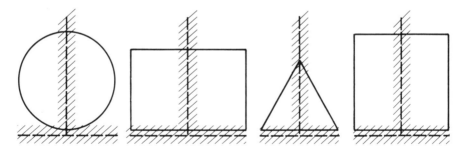

FIGURE 2.19

felt axis is naturally more difficult to establish, yet the process still gives maximum importance compositionally. Thus a visual element placed in the felt axis locus of the examples in Figure 2.20 is automatically emphasized. These are simple examples of what still holds true,

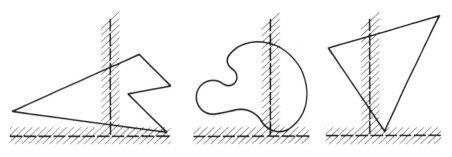

FIGURE 2.20

not only in complex shapes but also in complicated compositions. Yet no matter how involved the elements, the eye seeks out the felt axis in any visual event in an unending process of establishing the relative balance. In a triptych, the visual information set in the central panel takes compositional precedence over that in the lateral panels. The axis area of any field is looked at first; it is where you expect to see something. The same holds true for visual information in the lower half of any field, the eye being drawn to that locus in the secondary step of establishing balance through the horizontal reference.

LEVELING AND SHARPENING

But the power of the predictable pales before the power of surprise. Harmony and stability are polarities of the visually unexpected and stressful in composition. In psychology, these opposites are called leveling and sharpening. In a rectangular visual field, a simple demonstration of leveling would be to place a dot in the field in the dead center of a structural map (2.21). The placement of the dot as shown in Figure 2.22 offers no visual surprise; it is totally harmonious. Placement

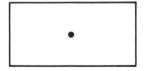

FIGURE 2.21   FIGURE 2.22

of the dot in the right-hand corner demonstrates sharpening (2.23). The dot is off center not only in the vertical structure but also in the horizontal structure as shown in Figure 2.24. It does not even conform to the diagonal components of the structural map (2.25). In either case, compositional leveling or sharpening, there is clarity of de-

FIGURE 2.23   FIGURE 2.24   FIGURE 2.25

sign. Through our automatic perceptions, we can establish balance or the marked lack of it, we can easily recognize the abstract visual conditions. But there is a third state of a visual composition which is neither leveled nor sharpened, where the eye must struggle to analyze the components as to their balance. This is called ambiguity and although the connotation is the same as in language, the form may be slightly differently described visually. The dot in Figure 2.26 is not clearly on center, nor is it far off-center as shown in Figure 2.27. Vi-

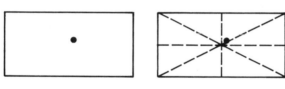

FIGURE 2.26   FIGURE 2.27

sually, its placement is unclear and would confound the viewer unconsciously hoping to stabilize its position in terms of relative balance. Visual ambiguity, like verbal ambiguity, obscures not only compositional intent, but also meaning. The natural balancing process would be slowed down, confused, and, most important, unresolved by the meaningless spatial phraseology of Figure 2.26. The Gestalt law of perceptual simplicity is greatly frustrated by such an unclear state of difference in all visual composition. In terms of sound visual syntax, ambiguity is totally undesirable. Of all our senses, sight is the one that wastes the least energy. It experiences and recognizes balance, obvious or subtle, and the interacting relationships of diverse visual data. It would be counterproductive to frustrate and confuse this unique function. Ideally, visual forms should not be purposefully unclear; they should harmonize or contrast, attract or repel, relate or clash.

PREFERENCE FOR LOWER LEFT
In addition to being influenced by elemental relationships to the structural map, visual stress is maximized two other ways: the eye fa-

vors the left-hand and lower area of any visual field. Translated into a
diagrammatic demonstration, this means that there is a primary scanning pattern of the field that responds to the vertical-horizontal referents (2.28) and a secondary scanning pattern that responds to the
left-lower perceptual pull (2.29).

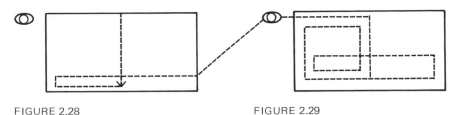

FIGURE 2.28   FIGURE 2.29

The explanations for these secondary perceptual preferences are many,
and they are not as easy to explain conclusively as primary preferences.
The favoring of the left part of the visual field could be influenced by
the Western print formation and the fact that there is strong conditioning in the way we learn to read from left to right. There is little
research and a great deal to be learned about why we are predominantly right-handed organisms and specialize our left-to-right reading
and writing competencies to the left hemisphere of the brain. Oddly,
right-handedness extends to cultures that have written from top to
bottom and presently write from right to left. We also favor the left
field of vision. If we do not know for sure why, it may be sufficient
to know that the fact does prove out in practice. Watch the eyes of
an audience scan a stage on which there is no action when the curtain
goes up in a theater.

SOME EXAMPLES

Conjecture though it may be, the fact of top-bottom, left-right weight
differences has great value in compositional decisions. It can give a refined knowledge of our understanding of stress as illustrated by Figure 2.30, which shows a linear division of a rectangle in a leveled composition; Figure 2.31 demonstrates sharpening but with minimized

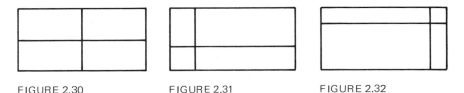

FIGURE 2.30   FIGURE 2.31   FIGURE 2.32

stress, while Figure 2.32 shows maximum stress. Of course, these facts may be modified for left-handed people or those who read their language any way other than left to right.

When visual material conforms to our expectations in terms of the felt axis, the horizontal stabilizing base, the dominance of the left-hand area of the field over the right, the lower half of the visual field over the upper half, we have a leveled composition, with minimum stress. When the opposite conditions obtain, we have a visual composition of maximum stress. In simple terms, the visual elements that are placed in areas of stress have more weight (2.33, 2.34, 2.35) than those that are leveled. Weight, which means in this context ability to attract the eye, of course, has enormous significance here in terms of compositional balance.

 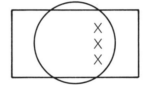

FIGURE 2.33   FIGURE 2.34   FIGURE 2.35

A practical demonstration of the theory demonstrated in Figure 2.36 shows that in a still life, one apple on the right balances two apples on the left. The compositional dominance is intensified by moving the right-hand apple higher than the two left-hand apples as shown in Figure 2.37.

FIGURE 2.36

FIGURE 2.37

Shapes have more weight or dominance visually in direct relationship to their relative regularity. Complexity, instability, irregularity increase visual stress and consequently attract the eye as shown in the regular shapes (2.38, 2.39, 2.40) and the irregular shapes (2.41, 2.42, 2.43). The two groups represent the choice between two major categories in composition: the balanced, rational, harmonious, as opposed to the exaggerated, distorted, and emotional.

In Gestalt theory of perception, the law of Prägnanz defines psychological organization as being as "good" (regular, symmetrical, simple) as prevailing conditions allow. "Good," in this case, is not a desirable or even very descriptive word, considering the intended meaning; a more accurate definition would be emotionally least provoking, sim-

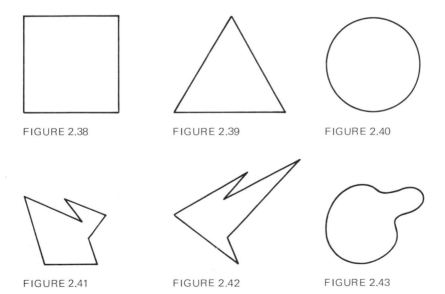

FIGURE 2.38   FIGURE 2.39   FIGURE 2.40

FIGURE 2.41   FIGURE 2.42   FIGURE 2.43

plest, least complicated, all of which describe the state arrived at visually through bilateral symmetry. Axial balance designs are not only easy to understand, they are easy to do, employing the least complicated formulation of counterpoise. If a dot is placed firmly to the left of the vertical or felt axis, a state of imbalance is provoked as shown in Figure 2.44 and immediately countered by the addition of another dot on balance in Figure 2.45. This is a perfect demonstration of counterpoise, which, when used in a visual composition, produces the most ordered and organized effect possible. The classic Greek temple is a tour de force in symmetry and, as would be expected, a most serene visual form.

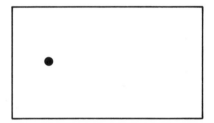   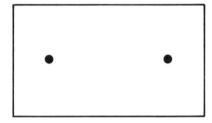

FIGURE 2.44   FIGURE 2.45

It is exceptional to find much in nature or the work of man that can reach an idealized state of balance. It could be argued that it is compositionally more dynamic to arrive at a balance of the elements in a visual work through the technique of asymmetry. It is not as easy. Variations of the visual means involve factors of compositional weight, size, and position. Figures 2.46 and 2.47 demonstrate the axial distribution of weight based on size. It is also quite possible to balance dissimilar weights by shifting their position as shown in Figure 2.48.

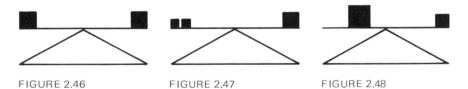

FIGURE 2.46   FIGURE 2.47   FIGURE 2.48

ATTRACTION AND GROUPING
The power of attraction in visual relationships represents another Gestalt principle with great compositional value, the law of grouping. It has two levels of significance to the visual language. It is a visual

condition that creates a circumstance of give and take of relative interaction. A dot alone in a field relates to the whole as shown in Figure 2.49, but it stands alone, and the relationship is a mild state of in-
termodification between it and the square. In Figure 2.50, the two
dots fight for attention in their interaction, creating comparatively individual statements because of their distance from one another and,
consequently, appearing to repel each other. In Figure 2.51, there is
an immediate and more intense interaction; the dots harmonize and,
therefore, attract each other. The closer they are, the stronger their
attraction. In the spontaneous act of seeing, individual visual units

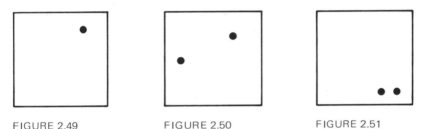

FIGURE 2.49   FIGURE 2.50   FIGURE 2.51

create other and distinct shapes. The closer the marks the more complicated the forms they can describe. In simple diagrams like 2.52 and
2.53 the eye supplies the missing connective links. Man, through his
perceptions, has a need to make wholes of units, in this case, to connect the dots by responding to their attraction. This is the visual phe-

FIGURE 2.52

nomenon that inspired ancient man to see the interacting points of
light of the stars as representational forms. We still can do the same
thing on a clear, starry night when we look up at the sky and make
out those forms of Orion or the Big and Little Dipper, recognized so
long ago. One might even try an original exercise in finding objects
described by the encompassing light dots of the stars.

The second level of importance to visual literacy of the law of grouping is how it is affected by similarity. In visual language, opposites re-

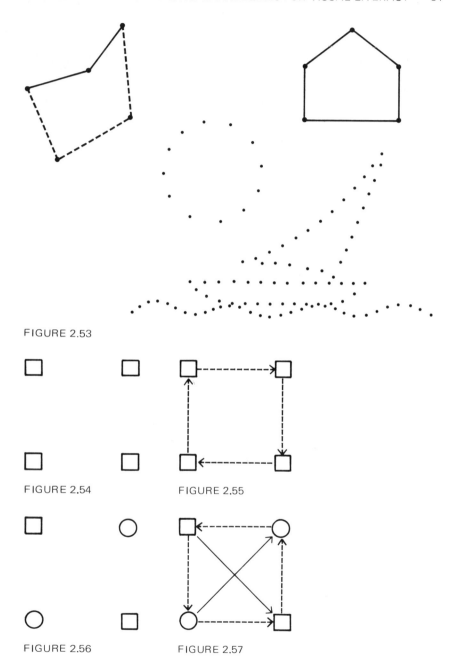

FIGURE 2.53

FIGURE 2.54   FIGURE 2.55

FIGURE 2.56   FIGURE 2.57

pel, but similars attract. So the eye fills in the missing connections but automatically relates the like units more strongly. The perceptual process is demonstrated by the visual clues of Figure 2.54, which create a square (2.55). But in Figure 2.56, the clues have been changed and their shape influences what elements are connected and in what order; Figure 2.57 shows the possible connections. In all four figures (2.54-2.57) the similarity demonstrated is shape, but many other visual affinities govern the law of grouping in the act of seeing, such as size, texture, or tone, as shown in Figures 2.58, 2.59, and 2.60.

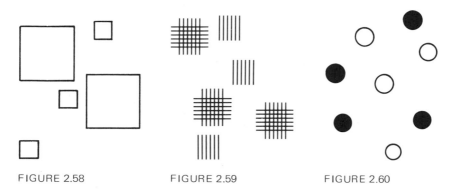

FIGURE 2.58   FIGURE 2.59   FIGURE 2.60

POSITIVE AND NEGATIVE

All that we see has the grammatical quality of being the major state-ment or the modifier—in verbal terminology, the noun or the adjec-tive. This structural relationship in the visual message has a strong connection to the sequence of seeing and absorbing information. A square is a good example of a field that is a positive visual statement clearly expressing its own definition and character and quality (2.61). It would be fair to observe that, as in the case of most of these exam-ples, the square is the simplest possible field. The introduction of a dot onto the square or field (2.62), although it, too, is an uncomplica-ted visual element, sets up visual tension, stress, and absorbs the visu-al attention of the viewer away from the square in some part. It sets up a sequence of seeing which is called positive and negative seeing. The significance of positive and negative in this context means mere-ly that there are separate yet unified elements in all visual events. Fig-ures 2.62 and 2.63 demonstrate that positive and negative are in no way meant to describe darkness or lightness or mirror image as they do in the description of film and prints in photography. Whether it is a dark dot on a light field as in Figure 2.62 or a white dot on a dark ground as in 2.63, the dot is the positive form, the active stress, and the square the negative form. In other words, what dominates the eye in visual experience would be considered the positive elements while those more passively displayed would be considered the negative. Posi-

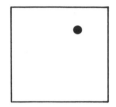

FIGURE 2.61   FIGURE 2.62   FIGURE 2.63

tive and negative seeing can sometimes fool the eye. You look at something and in the visual clues see what is not there. Two couples huddling in the distance appear to be a dog on its haunches. A face can appear to us in the shape of a stone. Involvement with relative and active clues of seeing an object can sometimes be so convincing that it is almost impossible to see what you are really looking at. This trick of the eye has always been of great interest to Gestaltists. In Figure 2.64, the positive-negative sequence is demonstrated by whether you see a vase or two profiles, which you see first, if, in fact, you see them both. The same observations could be made of how you see the juxtaposed 2 and 3 in Figure 2.65. In both examples there is little dominance of one element over the other, which reinforces the ambiguity of the visual statement. The eye seeks one simple solution to what it is seeing, and, although the process of assimilating the information may be long and complicated, simplicity is the end sought. The Chinese symbol of yin-yang, shown in Figure 2.66, is a perfect example of simultaneous contrast and complementary design. Like the "arch which never sleeps," the yin-yang is dynamic in both its simplicity and complexity, constantly moving; its negative-positive visual state is never resolved. It is as close a balance of individual elements brought together into a cohesive whole as one can find.

There are other examples of psychophysical facts of seeing that can be utilized in the understanding of visual language. What is larger ap-

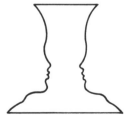

FIGURE 2.64   FIGURE 2.65   FIGURE 2.66

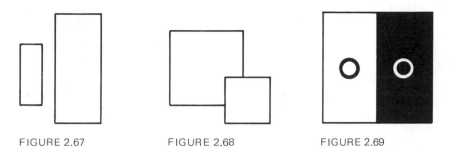

FIGURE 2.67   FIGURE 2.68   FIGURE 2.69

pears to be closer in the field, as shown in Figure 2.67. Yet, relative distance is even more distinctly legislated by overlap (2.68). Light elements on a dark ground appear to expand while dark elements on a light ground appear to contract (2.69).

There is a Berlitz approach to visual communication. You don't have to decline verbs or spell words or learn syntax. You learn by doing. In the visual mode you pick up a pencil or crayon and you draw; you doodle out a rough plan for a new living room; you paint a sign announcing a public event. You can negotiate the visual means to make a message or a plan or an interpretation, but how does the effort fit in terms of visual literacy? The major differences between the direct, intuitive approach and visual literacy is the level of dependability and accuracy between the message encoded and the message received. In verbal communication what is spoken is heard only once. Knowing how to write affords a greater chance for control of effect and narrows the area of interpretation. So, also, with a visual message, but not quite. The complexity of the visual mode does not allow the narrow range of interpretation of language. But in-depth knowledge of the perceptual processes that govern response to visual stimuli increases the control of meaning.

The examples in this chapter are only part of the possible visual information that can be utilized in developing a visual language anyone can articulate and understand. Knowing these facts of perception educates our compositional plan and affords syntactical guidelines to those seeking a beginning toward achieving visual literacy. The standards of literacy do not require that every verbal message-maker be a poet; therefore, it seems only fair that every designer or maker of visual material need not be a great and talented artist. This is a beginning toward releasing the ability of a generation immersed in a highly visual media environment; here are the ground rules that can serve as a strategic syntax for the visually illiterate to control and legislate the content of their visual work.

EXERCISES

1. Photograph or find an example of perfect balance and an example of complete imbalance. Analyze them from the point of view of the basic compositional arrangement and its effects, particularly its meaning.

2. Do a collage using two different shapes as the means for identifying and associating two separate groups (such as old/young, rich/poor, happy/sad).

3. Find an example of a bad visual design in graphics, which, although it was intended to deliver a message, is difficult to read and understand. Analyze how much ambiguity has contributed to the failure of the visual statement. Roughly resketch the design (1) to level the effect and (2) to sharpen the effect.

3
THE BASIC ELEMENTS OF VISUAL COMMUNICATION

Whenever anything is designed and made, sketched and painted, drawn, scratched, constructed, sculpted, or gestured, the visual substance of the work is composed from a basic list of elements. Visual elements are not to be confused with the materials or a medium, the wood or clay or paint or film. The visual elements are the basic substance of what we see, and they are few in number: the dot, line, shape, direction, tone, color, texture, dimension, scale, movement. Few though they may be, they comprise the raw material of all visual information in selective choices and combinations. The structure of the visual work is the force that determines which visual elements are present and with what emphasis.

Much of what we know about the interaction and effect of human perception on visual meaning is drawn from the research and experimentation in Gestalt psychology, but Gestalt thinking has more to offer than just the relationship between psychophysiological phenomena and visual expression. Its theoretical base is the belief that an approach to understanding and analyzing all systems requires recognizing that the system (or object or event, et cetera) as a whole is made up of interacting parts, which can be isolated and viewed as completely independent and then reassembled into the whole. No one unit of the system can be changed without modifying the whole. Any visual event or work is an incomparable example of this thesis since it was originally devised to exist as a well-balanced and inextricably involved totality. You can analyze any visual work from many points of view; one of the most revealing is to break it down into its constituent elements to better understand the whole. This process can provide deep insights into the nature of any visual medium as well as that of the individual work and the previsualization and making of a visual statement as well as the interpretation and response to it.

Using the basic visual components as a means for knowledge and understanding of either complete categories of visual media or individual works is an excellent method for exploration of their potential and realized success in expression. Dimension, for instance, exists as a visual element in architecture and sculpture and in both these media is dominant in relation to other visual elements. The whole science and art of perspective was developed during the Renaissance to suggest the presence of dimension in two-dimensional visual work such as painting and drawing. Even with the trompe d'oeil aid of perspec-

tive, dimension in these visual forms can only be implied, not expressed. But nowhere is dimension more subtly and completely synthesized than in film, still and moving. The lens sees as the eye sees in
complete detail, fully reinforced with all of the visual elements. All
of which is another way of saying the visual elements are richly present in our natural environment. No such completeness of replication
of our visual setting is present in the beginnings of visual ideas, the
plan, the rough sketch. Previsualization is dominated by the simple,
spare, yet highly expressive element of line.

It is vital to note here that the choice of emphasis of visual elements,
the manipulation of those elements toward an intended effect, lies in
the hands of artist and craftsman and designer; he is the visualizer.
What he chooses to do with them is his art and craft, and the choices
are infinite. The simplest visual elements can be used with great complexity of intention: the dot juxtaposed in varying sizes is the integral element of the halftone print and plate (cut), which is the mechanical means for mass reproduction of continuous tone visual material, particularly photographs; at the same time, the photograph, whose
character it is to report the environment in exact visual detail, can become a simplifying and abstract medium in the hands of a master photographer like Aaron Siskind. Deeper understanding of the elemental
construction of visual forms offers the visualizer greater freedom and
options in composition; those options are essential to the visual communicator.

To analyze and understand the total structure of a visual language, it
is helpful to focus on the individual visual elements, one at a time, so
as to better understand their unique qualities.

THE DOT
The dot is the simplest, irreducibly minimum unit of visual communication. In nature, roundness is the most common formulation, the
straight or square in the natural state being a rarity. When any liquid
material is dropped on a surface, it assumes a rounded form, even if
it does not simulate a perfect dot. When we make a mark, whether
with color or heavy substance or with a stick, we think of that visual
element as a dot that can serve as a reference point or a marker of
space. Any point has strong visual power to attract the eye wherever
it exists naturally or is placed by man in response to a purpose (3.1).

Two dots serve as handy tools for measuring space in the environment or in the development of any kind of visual plan (3.2). We learn

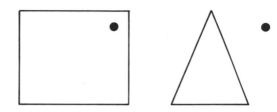

FIGURE 3.1

early to utilize the dot as the ideal notation system in conjunction with the ruler and other measurement devices such as the compass. The more complex the measurements necessary in a visual plan, the more dots are employed (3.3, 3.4).

FIGURE 3.2   FIGURE 3.3   FIGURE 3.4

When seen, dots connect and therefore are capable of leading the eye (3.5). In great profusion and juxtaposed, dots create the illusion of tone or color, which, as already noted, is the visual fact on which the mechanical means for reproducing any continuous tone is based (3.6, 3.7). The perceptual phenomenon of visual fusion was explored by Seurat in his Pointillist paintings, which are remarkably varied in color and tone, although he used only four pots of paint—yellow, red, blue, and black—and applied the paint with tiny, pointed brushes. All the Impressionists explored the process of blending, contrasting, and organizing, which took place in the eyes of the viewer. Involving and exciting, the process was in some ways similar to some of the more re-

FIGURE 3.5   FIGURE 3.6   FIGURE 3.7

cent theories of McLuhan concerning visual involvement and participation in the act of seeing as a part of the meaning. But no one
probed the possibilities as completely as Seurat, who, in his efforts,
seems to have anticipated four-color halftone process by which almost all full-color continuous-tone photographs and drawings are now
reproduced in mass printing.

The unique ability of a series of dots to lead the eye is intensified the
closer the dots are to one another (3.8).

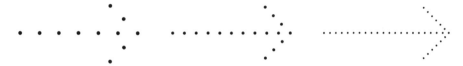

FIGURE 3.8

THE LINE
When the dots are so close to one another that they cannot be individually recognized, the sensation of direction is increased, and the
chain of dots becomes another distinctive visual element, a line (3.9).
A line could also be defined as a dot in motion, or the history of a
dot's movement, since, when we make a continuous mark or a line,
we make it by placing a marker point on a surface and moving it
along, leaving the formed marks as a record (3.10).

FIGURE 3.9

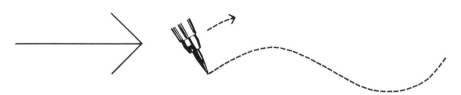

FIGURE 3.10

In the visual arts, line, because of its nature, has enormous energy. It is never static; it is the restless, probing, visual element of the sketch. Line, wherever it is employed, is the essential tool of previsualization, the means for presenting in palpable form that which does not exist yet, except in the imagination. In this way, it is tremendously useful to the visual process. Its fluid linear quality contributes to the freedom of experimentation. Yet for all its looseness and freedom, line is not vague: it is decisive; it has direction and purpose, it is going somewhere, it is doing something definitive. Thus, line can also be tight and technical, serving as the prime element in diagrammatic plans for mechanical construction and architecture and many other highly measured or scaled visual representations. Whether it is used loosely and experimentally (3.11) or tightly and measured (3.12), line is the indispensable means for making visible what cannot be seen, what does not exist except in the imagination.

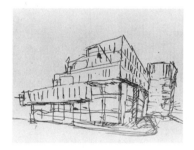

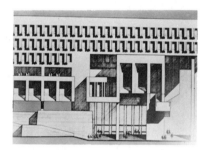

FIGURE 3.11   FIGURE 3.12

Line is also a tool for notation systems, writing, for example. Writing, map-making, electric symbols, and music are all examples of symbol systems in which line is the most important element. But in art, line is the essential element of the drawing, which is a notation system that does not stand for something else, symbolically, but does capsulize visual information, boiling it down to a state of reduction where all superfluous visual information has been stripped away and only the essential remains. This spareness has a highly dramatic effect in drawings or drypoints, woodcuts, etchings, and lithographs.

Line can take many different forms to express many different moods. It can be very loose and undisciplined, as in the sketches illustrated, to take advantage of its spontaneity of expression. It can be very deli-

cate and undulating or bold and coarse, even in the hands of the
same artist. It can be hesitant, indecisive, questioning, when it is merely a visual probe toward a design. It can also be as personal as hand-
writing in the form of nervous doodles, which are a hallmark of the
unconscious activity under the pressure of thinking or as amusement
in boredom. Even in the bloodless, mechanical format of maps, plans
for a house, cogs in a machine, line expresses the intention of the
maker and artist, and, further, his most personal feelings and emotions, and most important, his vision.

Line rarely exists in nature. But line does appear in the environment:
the crack in a sidewalk, telephone wires against the sky, bare branches in winter, a cable bridge. The visual element of line is used mostly
to express the juxtaposition of two tones. Line is utilized most often
to describe that juxtaposition, and in this, it is an artificial device.

SHAPE

Line describes shape. In the parlance of the visual arts, line articulates
the complexity of shape. There are three basic shapes, the square, circle, and equilateral triangle. Each of the basic shapes (3.13) has its
own unique character and characteristics and to each is attached a
great deal of meaning, some through association, some through arbitrary attached meaning, and some through our own psychological and
physiological perceptions. The square has associated to it dullness,
honesty, straightness, and workmanlike meaning; the triangle, action,
conflict, tension; the circle, endlessness, warmth, protection.

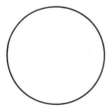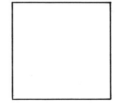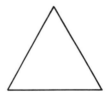

FIGURE 3.13

All the basic shapes are fundamental, simple planal figures, which can
be easily described and constructed either visually or verbally. A
square is a four-sided figure with exactly equal right angles at each
corner and sides of exactly the same length (3.14). A circle is a con-
tinuously curved figure whose outline is at all points equidistant from

its center point (3.15). An equilateral triangle is a three-sided figure whose angles and sides are all equal (3.16). From these basic shapes in endless combinations and variations, we derive all physical forms in nature and in the imagination of man (3.17).

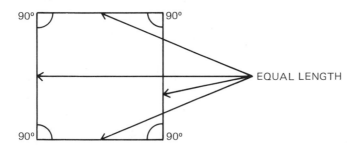

FIGURE 3.14

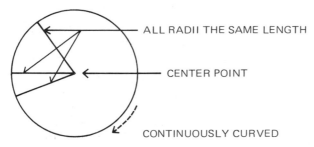

FIGURE 3.15

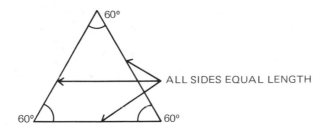

FIGURE 3.16

FIGURE 3.17

DIRECTION

Every basic shape expresses three basic and meaningful visual directions: the square, the horizontal and vertical (3.18): the triangle, diagonal (3.19); the circle, the curve (3.20). Each of the visual directions has strong associative meaning and is a valuable tool in making visual messages. The horizontal-vertical (3.21) reference has been commented on already, but to review, it is man's primary reference in terms of his well-being and maneuverability. Its most basic meaning has to do not only with the human organism's relationship to the environment, but also to stability in all visual matters. Not only does man have more ease in balance; so do all things constructed and designed. Diagonal direction (3.22) has particular significance in direct reference to the idea of stability. It is the opposite formulation, the most unstable directional force and consequently the most provoking visual formulation. Its meaning is threatening and almost literally upsetting. Curved directional forces (3.23) have meanings associated with

FIGURE 3.18   FIGURE 3.19   FIGURE 3.20

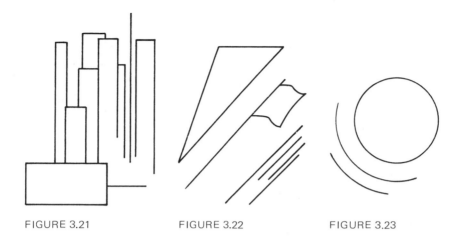

FIGURE 3.21   FIGURE 3.22   FIGURE 3.23

encompassment, repetition, and warmth. All directional forces have great importance to compositional intention toward final effect and meaning.

TONE

The edges that line is used to represent in a rough sketch or a detailed, mechanical plan in the environment, for the most part, appear as the juxtaposition of tone, the intensity of darkness or lightness of anything seen. We see because of the relative presence or absence of light, but light is not uniformly shed on the environment either by the sun or moon or by artificial light. If it were, we would be as much in the dark as we are in complete absence of light. Light goes around things, is reflected by shiny surfaces, falls on objects which themselves have relative lightness and darkness. Variations in light or tone are the means by which we optically distinguish the complicated visual information in the environment. In other words, we see what is dark because it abuts or overlaps what is light, and vice-versa (3.24, 3.25).

FIGURE 3.24   FIGURE 3.25

From dark to light in nature, there are multiple subtle steps which, in man's means for reproduction of nature in art and film, are severely limited. When we observe tonality in nature, we are seeing true light. When we talk of tonality in graphics, painting, photography, film, we have reference to some kind of pigment, paint, or nitrate of silver, which is used to simulate natural tone. Between light and dark in nature, there are hundreds of distinct tonal steps, but in graphic arts and photography these steps are severely limited (3.26). From white to black in pigment, the most commonly used tonal scale has about thirteen steps. At the Bauhaus and at many other art schools, students have always been challenged to see how many distinct and recognizable tonal steps they could represent from black to white. With great sensitivity and delicacy, they can be pushed to 30+ tones of gray, but this is not practical for common use since it is too subtle visually. How, then, can the visualizer cope with this tonal limitation? Manipulation of tone through juxtaposition greatly lessens the tonal limitations inherent in the problem of emulating the tonal largess of nature. One tone of gray can change dramatically when it is placed on a tonal scale (3.27). The possibility for highly expanded tonal representation can be achieved through utilization of these means.

FIGURE 3.26

FIGURE 3.27

The world we live in is dimensional, and tone is one of the visualizer's best tools for indicating and expressing that dimension. Perspective is the method for plotting many of the special visual effects in our natural surroundings, to represent the three-dimensional way we see in two-dimensional graphic form. It uses many devices to plot distance, bulk, point of view, the vanishing point, the horizon line, eye level, et cetera (3.28). But even with the aid of perspective, line alone will not create the illusion of reality effectively without the aid of tone (3.29). The addition of tonal background detail reinforces the appearance of reality through the sensation of reflected light and cast sha-

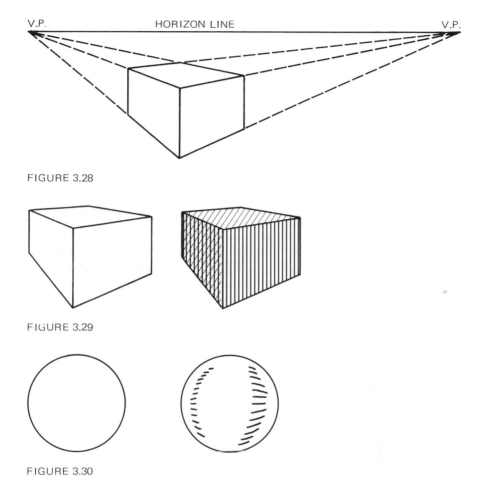

V.P.   HORIZON LINE   V.P.

FIGURE 3.28

FIGURE 3.29

FIGURE 3.30

dows. This effect is even more dramatic in simple, basic shapes such as the circle, which could not appear as dimensional without tonal information (3.30).

Lightness and darkness are so intensely important to the perception of our environment that we accept a monochromatic representation of reality in the visual arts and we do it without hesitation. In fact, the varying tones of gray in photographs, film, television, etching, mezzotints, tonal sketches, are monochromatic surrogates and represent a world that does not exist, a visual world we accept only because of the dominance of tonal values in our perceptions (Plate 3.1).*

*Plates 3.1-3.6 are on pages 53 and 54.

The ease with which we accept the monochromatic visual representation is the exact measure of just how vitally important tone is to us, and even more interesting, just how unconsciously sensitive we are to the dull, monochromatic values of our environment. How many people even realize they have this sensitivity? The reason for this startling visual fact is that tonal sensitivity is most basic to our survival. It is second only to the vertical-horizontal reference as visual clues to our relationship to our surroundings. Through it we see sudden movement, depth, distance, and other environmental references. Tonal value is another way of describing light. Through it, and only through it, we see.

COLOR

The monochromatic representations we so readily accept in the visual media are tonal stand-ins for color, for what is, in truth, a chromatic world, our richly colored universe. While tone is related to questions of survival and is therefore essential to the human organism, color has stronger affinity to the emotions. It is possible to think of color as the aesthetic frosting on the cake, rich, and in many ways useful, but not absolutely necessary for creating visual messages. That would be a very shallow view of the matter. Color is, in fact, loaded with information and one of the most pervasive visual experiences we all have in common. It is, therefore, an invaluable source for visual communicators. In the environment we share the associative meanings of the color of trees, grass, sky, earth and on endlessly to where we see color as a common stimulus. And there, we associate meaning. We know color also under a broad category of symbolic meaning. Red means something, for instance, even where it does not have any environmental connection. The red that is associated with anger has been carried over into the "red flag (or cape) waved in front of a bull." The color red has little significance for the bull, who has no sensitivity to the color, but only to the fact that the cape or flag moves. Red means danger, and love, and warmth, and life, and maybe a hundred other things. Each color has as many meanings, associative and symbolic. Thus, color offers an enormous vocabulary of great usefulness in visual literacy. The variety of meaning obtainable is expressed in this example from Carl Sandburg's poem, "The People, Yes":

The blood of all men of all nations being red
the Communist International named red its banner color
Pope Innocent IV gave cardinals their first red hats
saying a cardinal's blood belonged to the holy mother church.
The bloodcolor red is a symbol.

There are many color theories. Color, both the color of light and the color of pigment, behaves in unique ways, but our knowledge of color in visual communication goes very little further than collecting observations of our reactions to it. There is no single, ultimate system of how hues relate to each other.

Color has three dimensions which can be defined and measured. Hue is the color itself, or chroma, of which there are more than a hundred. Each hue has individual characteristics; groups or categories of colors share common effects. There are three primary or elementary hues: yellow, red, blue. Each represents qualities that are fundamental. Yellow is the color considered closest to light and warmth; red is the most emotional and active; blue is passive and soft. Yellow and red tend to expand, blue to contract. In association with each other, through mixtures, new meanings take over. Red, which is a provoking hue, is subdued when it is mixed with blue and activated when it is mixed with yellow. The same changes in effect are reached with yellow, which mellows when it is mixed with blue.

Color structure in its simplest formulation is taught through the color wheel. The primary colors, yellow, red, blue, and the secondary colors, orange, green, violet, are invariably included in such a chart. But it usually also includes expanded mixtures of at least twelve hues. From this simple chart of a color wheel (Plate 3.2), multiple variations of color hues can be developed.

The second dimension of color is saturation, which is the relative purity of a color from the hue to gray. Saturated color is simple, almost primitive, and always given preference by folk artists and children. It is both uncomplicated and overstated, composed of the primary and secondary hues. The less saturated colors reach toward neutrality of color, even noncolor, and are subtle and restful. The more intense or saturated the coloration of a visual object or event, the more highly charged it is with expression and emotion. Informational results in the choice of saturated or neutralized color base choice on intention. But saturation or its absence as a meaningful visual effect is the difference between the dentist's office and the Electric Circus.

The third, and last dimension of color is achromatic. It is the relative brightness, from light to dark, of value or tonal gradations. It must be noted, underlined, and emphasized that the presence or absence of color does not affect tone; it is constant. A color television set is an excellent device for demonstrating this visual fact. When you turn the color knob slowly to black and white, to the monochromatic picture, you slowly drain off the color saturation. The process in no way affects the tonal values of the picture. Turning the saturation up and down demonstrates the constancy of tone and proves that color and tone coexist in perception without modifying each other.

An afterimage is the physiological visual phenomenon that takes place after the human eye has been fixed or focused on any visual information. When the object or information being stared at is replaced with a blank white field, a negative image is seen on the blank space. The effect is related to the spots one sees after flash bulbs or bright lights are directed into the eye. Although this is an extreme example, any visual material or tone will cause an afterimage. The negative afterimage of a color produces the complementary color or its exact opposite. It is on this visual phenomenon that Munsell based the entire structure of his color theory. The opposite color on his color wheel is what the afterimage would be. But there are further implications of what happens when you stare at a color long enough to produce an afterimage. You will first see the complementary color. For instance, if you stare at yellow, purple will appear on the blank area in your afterimage (Plate 3.3). Yellow is the closest hue to white or light; purple the closest to black or dark. The afterimage in Plate 3.3 will not only be tonally darker than the value of yellow, but will be the median tone of gray, if they were mixed or balanced (Plate 3.4). A red of a middle tonal value would produce a complementary green of the same middle tone. The afterimage, then, appears to react in the same tonal fashion as pigment. When you mix two complementary colors together, red and green, yellow and purple, they not only cancel out each other's chroma or hue to gray, they also produce from their mixture a middle tone of gray.

There is another way of demonstrating this process. Two complementary colors displayed on the same middle tone of gray affect the neutral tone. The gray panel with a warm, red-orange hue appears bluish or cool (Plate 3.5), while the reverse occurs with the gray on which a blue-green square is displayed (Plate 3.6). Its gray background appears reddish-toned and warm. This experiment shows that the eye is seeing the opposite or contrasting hue, not just in the afterimage, but at the same time it is viewing a color. The process is called "simultaneous contrast," and its psychophysiological significance extends beyond just its importance to color theory. It is another piece of evidence that indicates the intense need to reach for complete neutrality and hence

Plate 3.1

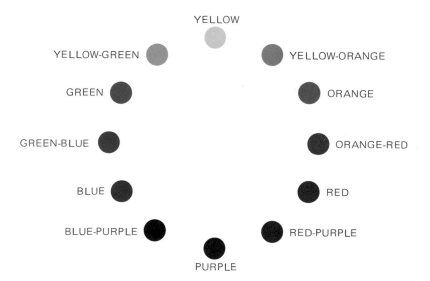

Plate 3.2

Plate 3.3

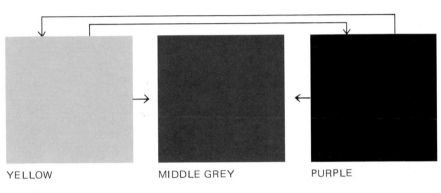

YELLOW   MIDDLE GREY   PURPLE

Plate 3.4

Plate 3.5

Plate 3.6

complete repose that man demonstrates over and over again in the visual context.

Since perception of color is the single most strongly emotional part of the visual process, it has great force and can be utilized to express and reinforce visual information to great advantage. Color not only has universally shared meaning through experience, but it also has separate worth informationally through symbolically attached meaning. In addition to the highly negotiable color meaning, each of us has our own personal and subjective color preferences. We choose our own color statements and settings. But there is little analytic thought or concern about what methods or motivation we use to arrive at our own choices in terms of the meaning and effect of color. When a jockey dons an owner's silks, a soldier wears his dress uniform, a nation displays its flag, the attempt to find symbolic meaning in their colors may be obvious. Not so in our personal color choices, which are less symbolic and therefore less clearly defined. Nevertheless, whether we think about it or not, realize it or not, we tell the world a great deal when we make a color choice.

TEXTURE
Texture is the visual element that frequently serves as a stand-in for the qualities of another sense, touching. But, in fact, we can appreciate and recognize texture either by touch or sight individually, or by a combination of both. It is possible for a texture to have no tactile quality, only optical, like the lines of type on a printed page, or polka dots on material, or crosshatched lines in a doodle. Where there is actual texture, the tactile and optical qualities coexist, not like tone and color which are unified in their comparable and even value, but separately and uniquely, affording individual sensation to the eye and the hand, even though we project onto both strong associative meaning. What sandpaper looks like and what sandpaper feels like have the same intellectual meaning, but not the same value. They are singular experiences which may or may not suggest each other under certain circumstances. The judgment of the eye is usually checked on by the hand by actual touching. Is it really smooth or does it just look that way? Is that an indentation or a raised mark? No wonder there are so many "do not touch" signs!

Texture has reference to the composition of a substance through minute variations on the surface of the material. Texture should serve as a sensitive and enriching experience. Unfortunately, those "do not touch" signs in the expensive shops overlap into social behavior, and we are strongly conditioned not to touch things or people with anything approximating sensual involvement. The result is a minimal tactile experience and even a fear of tactile contact; the sense of blind touch is carefully guarded in sighted people. We act super-cautiously when blindfolded or in the dark, reaching out tentatively, and, because of our limited experience of touch, we often do not recognize a texture. At the 1967 Montreal Expo, the 5+ Comingo Pavilion was designed for visitors to explore the quality of their five senses. It was a popular and enjoyable exhibit. People sniffed away at a series of funnels offering a variety of odors, even though they suspected, and justifiably, that some would be unpleasant. They listened, they looked, tasted, but they stood hesitant and inhibited in front of the yawning holes designed to be reached into blindly. What did they fear? It appears that the natural, free, "hands on" investigative approach of the baby and young child has been conditioned out of the adult by—Who knows what?—the Anglo-Saxon ethic, Puritan repression, instinctive taboos. Whatever the reason, the result starves one of our richest senses. But in this increasingly simulated and plastic world, the problem arises infrequently. Most of our textural experience is optical, not tactile. Not only is texture faked rather convincingly in plastics and printed material and faked fur, but, also, much of what we see that is painted, photographed, and filmed convincingly presents texture that is not there. If we touch a photograph of silky velvet, we do not have the convincing tactile experience the visual clues promise. Meaning is based on what we see. This fakery is an important factor in survival in nature; animals, birds, reptiles, insects, fish, take on the coloration and texture of their surroundings as a protection against predators. Man copies this camouflage method in war in response to the same needs for survival that inspires it in nature.

SCALE

All visual elements have the capacity to modify and define each other. The process, itself, is the element of scale. Color is bright or subdued depending on juxtaposition, just as relative tonal values take on enormous visual modifications depending on what tone is next to or behind them. In other words, there can be no large without small (3.31). But even when large is established through small, the entire scale can be changed with the addition of another visual modification (3.32). Scale can be established not only through the relative size of visual clues, but also through relationships to the field or the environment. The visual results in terms of scale are fluid and not absolute, since

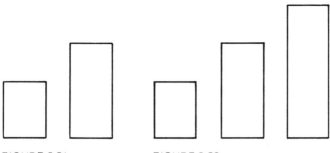

FIGURE 3.31   FIGURE 3.32

they are subject to so many variables of modification. In Figure 3.33, the square can be considered large because of its size relationship to the field, while the square in Figure 3.34 can be called small because of its relative size in the field. All that is being observed is true in the context of scale, false in terms of measurement, since the square in Figure 3.33 is smaller than the square in Figure 3.34.

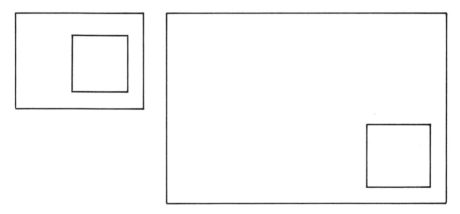

FIGURE 3.33   FIGURE 3.34

Scale is often used in plans and maps to represent real measurement in proportion. The scale is usually designated, for example, 1 inch = 100 miles, or 1 inch = 10 miles. The globe of the world represents enormous distance in small measurement. All of which requires some extension of understanding to visualize in terms of distance real measurement as it is simulated in a map or plan. Measurement is an integral part of scale, but it is not crucial. What is more important is juxtaposition, what is alongside of the visual subject, what setting it is in; these factors are more important.

The most vital factor in the establishment of scale is the measurement of man himself. In matters of design that relate to comfort and fit, all manufacture is geared to the average size of human proportion. There is an ideal proportion, a mean average, and all the endless variations that make us all unique. Mass production is, of course, ruled by the mean average with all large objects of manufacture, such as cars and bathtubs, adapted to that measure. On the other hand, clothes have multiple sizes in mass production, recognizing the enormous variations in individual human size.

There are proportional formulas on which scale can be based; the most famous is the Greek "Golden Mean." This is a mathematical formula of great visual elegance. It is arrived at by bisecting a square and using the diagonal of one half of the square as a radius to extend the dimensions of the square to become a "Golden Rectangle." In the proportion arrived at, a:b = c:a. The method of constructing the proportion is demonstrated in Figure 3.35 and Figure 3.36. The "Golden Mean" was used by the Greeks to design most of what they built from the classic Greek amphora to the floor plans of temples and their elevations (3.37, 3.38).

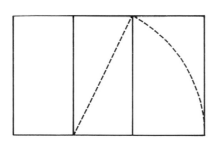

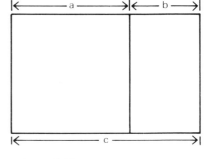

FIGURE 3.35   FIGURE 3.36

There are many other scale systems; the most outstanding contemporary version is that developed by the late French architect, Le Corbusier. His modular unit, on which his entire system is based, is the size of man, and on this proportion, he establishes an average ceiling height, door size, window opening, et cetera. Everything becomes unitized and repeatable. Oddly enough, the unitized system of mass production has these effects built into it, and creative design solutions are often limited by what is available to design with, a limiting factor.

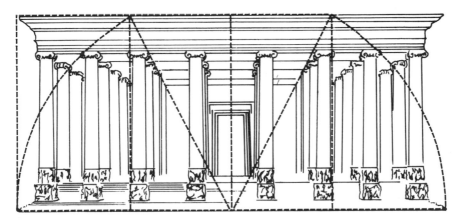

FIGURE 3.37

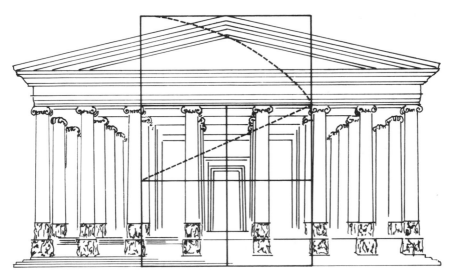

FIGURE 3.38

Learning to relate size to purpose and meaning is essential in the structuring of visual messages. Control of scale can make a large room seem
small and cozy and a small room appear open and airy. This effect
can extend to all manipulation of space, illusory though it may be.

DIMENSION

Representation of dimension in two-dimensional visual formats is also
dependent on illusion. Dimension exists in the real world. We cannot

only feel it, but, with the aid of our two-eyed, stereopticon sight, we can see it. But in all two-dimensional representations of reality in drawing, painting, photography, film, television, there is no actualized dimension, it is only implied. The illusion is reinforced in many ways, but the prime device for simulating dimension is the technical convention of perspective. The effects produced by perspective can be reinforced by tonal manipulation through "chiaroscuro," the dramatic emphasis of light and shade.

Perspective has exact formulas with many and complicated rules. It uses line to plot its effects, but its final intention is to produce the feeling of reality. There are some fairly easy rules and methods which can be demonstrated. Showing how two planes of a cube appear to the eye depends first, as shown in Figure 3.39, on establishing the eye level. There is only one vanishing point to which one plane disappears. The top cube is seen in a worm's eye view, while the bottom cube is seen in a bird's-eye view.

In Figure 3.40, two vanishing points must be used to express the perspective of a cube with three surfaces in sight. These are two extremely simple demonstrations of how perspective works. To present it adequately would take an enormous amount of explanation. The artist certainly does not use perspective slavishly. He uses it; he knows it. Ideally, the technical facts of perspective are in his mind because of careful study, and can be utilized in quite a free way.

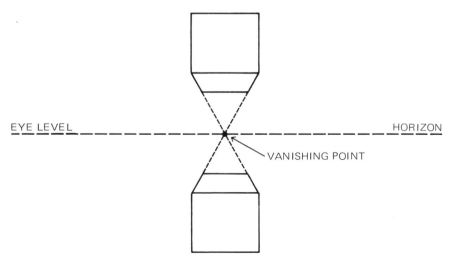

FIGURE 3.39

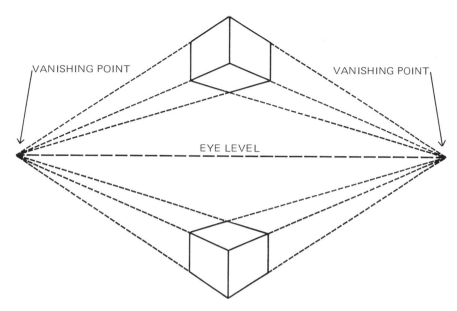

FIGURE 3.40

In photography, perspective dominates. The lens has some of the same properties as the eye, and simulation of dimension is one of its prime abilities. But there are some crucial modifications. The eye has wide peripheral vision (3.41), which the camera cannot duplicate.

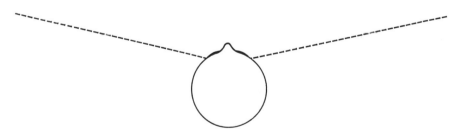

FIGURE 3.41

The scope of field of the camera lens is changeable, that is, what it can see and record is determined by the focal length of its lens. But it cannot match the eye without the enormous distortion of a fish-eye lens. The normal lens (3.43) has nowhere near the range of field of the eye, but what it does see is close to the perspective of the eye. The telephoto lens (3.42) can record visual information in ways the eye cannot, collapsing space like an accordion. The wide angle lens

broadens the scope of the field, but covers nowhere near the area of
the eyes (3.44). Even though we may observe of the camera that it
has its own perspective different from the human eye, one thing is
certain: the camera can replicate the environment with startling accuracy and in infinite detail.

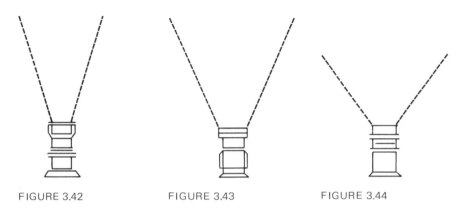

FIGURE 3.42   FIGURE 3.43   FIGURE 3.44

Real dimension is the dominating element in industrial design, crafts,
sculpture, architecture, and any visual material in which the total
and actual volume must be dealt with. This is enormously complex
and requires an ability to previsualize and plan in full dimension. The
difference in problem between the representation of volume in two
dimensions and the construction of the real thing in the full three dimensions can be best explained by Figure 3.45, where a piece of
sculpture is seen as a silhouetted shape augmented with some detail.
In 3.46, we see five views, top, front, back, right, left, of a piece of
sculpture. The five views represent only a few of the thousands of
silhouettes that the piece of sculpture contains. Paper-thin slices of
the sculpture would produce endless silhouetted drawings.

FIGURE 3.45

FIGURE 3.46

It is this extreme complexity of dimensional visualization that demands of the maker a tremendous grasp of the whole. Toward successful understanding of a problem, the design and planning of three-
dimensional visual material requires many steps to think through and
project the possible solutions. First, there is the sketch, usually in perspective. There may be endless sketches, loose and probing and uncommitted. Second, there are the working drawings which are rigid
and mechanical. The technical and engineering requirements of build-

FIGURE 3.47

ing or manufacture require these in careful detail. Last, though it is expensive, building a model (3.47) is probably the only way people with little sensitivity to visualization can be shown how something will appear in its completed form.

Despite the fact that our total human experience is set in a dimensional world, we tend to think of visualization as mark-making, and ignore the special problems of visual problem solving in terms of dimension.

MOVEMENT

The visual element of movement, like dimension, is more often implied in the visual mode than actually expressed. Yet movement is probably one of the most dominant visual forces in human experience. In actual fact, it exists only in film, television, the charming mobiles of Alexander Calder, and where something visualized and made has a movement component, like machinery or windows. But techniques can trick the eye; the illusion of texture or dimension appears real through the use of intense expression of detail, as in the case of texture, and the use of perspective and intensified light and shade as in the case of texture, and the use of perspective and intensified light and shade as in the case of dimension. Suggestion of motion in static visual statements is at once harder to achieve without distorting reality at the same time, implicit in everything we see. It derives from our complete experience of movement in life. In part, this implied action is projected into static visual information both psychologically and kinesthetically. After all, like the tonal world of achromatic film we accept so readily, the static forms of the visual arts are not natural to our experience. This stilled, frozen world is the best we could create, until the advent of the motion picture and its miracle of representing movement. But note, even in this form, true movement does not exist as we know it; it lies not in the medium, but in the eye of the beholder through the physiological phenomenon of "persistence of vision." Movie film is really a string of still pictures containing slight changes, which, when viewed by man in the proper time intervals, are blended together by a holdover factor in seeing so that the movement appears real.

Some of the properties of "persistence of vision" may be the incorrect reason for the use of the word, "movement," to describe compositional tensions and rhythms in visual data when what is being seen is fixed and unmoving. A painting, photograph, or fabric design may be static, but the amount of repose it projects compositionally may imply movement in response to the artist's design emphasis and intention. There is little rest in the process of seeing.

The eye is constantly scanning the environment in pursuit of the many methods it has for absorbing visual information. The formalized convention of reading, for instance, follows an organized sequence (3.48). Scanning, as a method of seeing, appears to be unstructured, yet, random though it may appear, research and measurement show that human scanning patterns are as individual and unique as fingerprints. It can be measured through the projection of a light into the eye and recording on film the reflection in the pupil as the eye looks at something (3.49). The eye also moves in response to the unconscious process of measurement and balance through the "felt axis" and left-right, top-bottom preferences (3.50). Since two or even all three of these visual methods may be going on at once, it is clear there is action not only in what is seen, but also in the process of seeing.

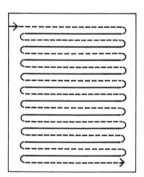

FIGURE 3.48

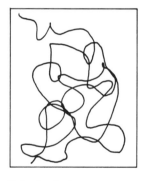

FIGURE 3.49

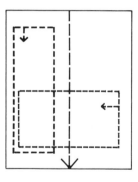

FIGURE 3.50

The miracle of motion as a visual component is dynamic. Man has used picture-making, form-making for many purposes, one of the most important of which is to objectify himself. No visual means has approached as complete and effective a mirror of man and his world as the motion picture.

All these elements, the dot, line, shape, direction, tone, color, texture, scale, dimension, movement, are the irreducible components of the visual media. They are the basic ingredients we draw on for the development of visual thinking and communication. They have the dramatic potential for carrying information with simple directness and ease, messages that are effortlessly understandable to anyone who who can see. These potentialities for conveying universal meaning universally have been recognized, but not pursued with the determination the situation demands. The instant information of television will make the world into a global village, says McLuhan. Yet language continues to dominate communication media. Language separates, nationalizes; the visual anneals. Language is complex and difficult; the visual is as fast as the speed of light and can instantaneously express many ideas. These basic elements are the essential visual means. Proper understanding of their character and workings is the basis for a language that will recognize no boundaries or barriers.

EXERCISES

1. In a 4-inch square, do a collage of any or all of the following individual visual elements: dot, line, texture. Each collage should be composed of many examples of the element as found in print or drawn and arranged so that the collage demonstrates some of the essential characteristics of the element.

2. In either a 4-inch square, a circle with a 4-inch diameter, or a triangle with a 4-inch base, compose a collage of objects or actions most often associated with that basic shape. The examples can be chosen from a magazine or other print materials or drawn. The composition should emphasize the quality of the particular shape.

3. Choose a sheet of colored paper, preferably a true shade produced by Color-Aid Paper, and on it draw or construct a collage that expresses one or more meanings that color has for you. Try to seek out some universal meaning for the color.

4. Photograph or design a collage that deliberately finds a familiar small object dwarfing an object we think of as large. The quality of surprise will demonstrate the strong predetermined sense of scale we all have.

5. Choose a photograph or painting of any subject and list the basic elements you can identify.

4

THE ANATOMY OF A VISUAL MESSAGE

We express and receive visual messages on three levels: representation-ally—what we see and recognize from environment and experience; abstractly—the kinesthetic quality of a visual event reduced to the basic elemental visual components, emphasizing the more direct, emotional, even primitive message-making means; symbolically—the vast world of coded symbol systems which man has created arbitrarily, and to which he has attached meaning. All these levels of information retrieval are interconnected and overlapping, but can be sufficiently distinguished from each other so that they can be analyzed both as to their value as potential tactics for message-making and their quality in the process of seeing.

Vision defines the act of seeing in all its ramifications. We see in sharp detail and learn and recognize all the elemental visual material in our lives in order to negotiate most competently in the world. This is our shared world of sky and sea, trees, grass, sand, earth, day, night; this is the world of nature. We see the world we make, a world of cities, airplanes, houses, machinery; this is the world of manufacture and the complexity of modern technology. We learn instinctively both to understand and maneuver psychophysiologically in the environment and intellectually to live with and operate those mechanical objects which are necessary to our survival. Both instinctively and intellectually, much of the learning process is visual. Sight is the only necessity for visual understanding. One does not need to be literate to speak or understand language; one need not be visually literate to make or understand visual messages. These abilities are intrinsic in man and will emerge, to some extent, with or without teaching or models. As they develop in history, so they develop in the child. The visual input is of profound importance to understanding and survival. Yet the whole area of vision has been compartmentalized and de-emphasized as a primary means for communication. One explanation of this rather negative approach is that visual talent and competency were not considered available to all people, as verbal literacy was thought to be. If this were ever true, it certainly is no longer. Part of the present and most of the future will be made by a generation conditioned by photography, film, and television, and to whom camera and visual computer will be an intellectual adjunct. One means of communication does not negate the other. If language can be compared with the visual mode, it must be understood that they are not in competition, but are merely to be weighed against each other in terms of effective-

ness and viability. Visual literacy has been and can be only an extension of man's unique message-making capacity.

Replication of natural visual information should be within the ability
of all. It should be taught. It can be learned. But it must be noted
that there is no external arbitrary structural system as there is in language. The hard information that exists lies within the syntactical
significance of the workings of the perceptions of the human organism. We see and what we see, we understand. Problem solving is inextricably connected with the visual mode. We can even reproduce the
visual information around us through the camera, and, what is more,
preserve it and extend it as simply as we have been able to through
writing and reading and, more importantly, through printing and
mass production of language. The difficult question is how. In what
way can visual communication be understood and learned and expressed? Up to the invention of the camera, this was primarily the
province of the artist, except for children and primitive people who
did not know they could not do it. For example, we can all see and
recognize a bird. We can extend this recognition to generalizing about
an entire species and its attributes. To some observers, the visual information reaches no further than a primary level of information. To
Leonardo da Vinci, a bird meant flying, and his investigation of that
fact led him to try to invent flying machines. We see a bird, maybe a
particular kind of bird, a dove, perhaps, and this has an extended
meaning of love or peace. The visionary does not stop at the obvious;
he sees beyond the surface visual facts into greater realms of meaning.

REPRESENTATION
Reality is the basic and dominating visual experience. The total general category of the bird is defined in elemental visual terms. A bird
can be identified through a general shape, linear and detailed characteristics. All birds have some connecting, shared visual referents within the broader category. But in highly representational terms, birds
fit into individual classifications, and knowledge of finer details of col-
or, proportion, size, movement, and markings is necessary to differen-
tiate between a seagull and a stork, a pigeon and a blue jay. One more
level is a factor in the identification of individual birds. A particular
canary may have individual visual traits that set it apart from the
whole category of canaries. The general idea of a bird with shared
characteristics moves toward the specific bird through increasingly detailed identifying factors. All this visual information is easily obtainable through various levels of the direct experience of seeing. We all

are the original camera; we all can store and recall for use this visual information with high visual effectiveness. The differences between the camera and the human brain lie in the questions of faithfulness of observation and ability to reproduce the visual information. It is clear that the artist and the camera hold some special expertise in both areas.

Beyond a realistic three-dimensional model, the closest thing to actually seeing a bird in direct experience would be a carefully exposed and focused photograph in full and natural color. The photograph matches the facility of the eye and brain, replicating the real bird in the real environment. We call the effect realistic. It should be noted, however, that in direct experience, or on any level of the scale of visual expression from photograph to impressionistic sketch, all visual experience is intensely subject to individual interpretation. From the "I see a bird" response to "I see flight," and to the multiple levels and degrees of meaning and intention between and beyond, the message is always open to subjective modification. We are all unique. Any inhibition about studying and even structuring the human visual potential born of a fear that such a development would lead to destruction of creative spirit, even conformity, is entirely without justification. Indeed, the mystique that has grown up around visualizers, from painters to architects, implies they must have a noncerebral approach to their work. The development of visual material should no more be dominated by inspiration and threatened by method than the converse. Making a film, designing a book, painting a painting, are all complicated ventures that must utilize both inspiration as well as method. Rules do not threaten creative thinking in mathematics; grammar and spelling do not impede creative writing. Coherence is not unaesthetic, and a well-expressed visual idea should have the same beauty and elegance as a mathematical theorem or a well-wrought sonnet.

The photograph is the most technically dependable means of representing visual reality. The invention of the "camera obscura" in the Renaissance as a toy for seeing the environment reproduced on wall or floor was only one step of a many branched tree that has made it possible through film and photography to arrive at the enormous and powerful effect the magic of the lens has had on our society. From the camera obscura to the mass media of film and printed photograph has been a slow but steady progression of more perfected technical means to fix and hold the picture and show it to millions the world over. Photography has been an accomplished fact for more than a hundred years. The many steps from the one, inclusive, nonreproducible "Daguerreotype" to the negative, multiple-print collotype, to flexible Kodak film, to 35 mm motion picture film, to the slowly improving methods of reproducing the continuous tone photograph through halftone plates for mass printing, to coated stock for finer printing—all have led to the pervasiveness of photography, both still and motion, in modern society. Through the photograph, an almost incomparably real, visual report of an occurrence in the daily printed newspaper or the weekly or monthly magazine, society sits shoulder to shoulder with history. The extension of this unique reportorial ability reaches into film, which even more accurately reproduces reality, and then to the electronic miracle of television, which allowed the world to share the first footstep of the first man on the moon, simultaneously with its occurrence. The concept of time was changed by mass printing; the concept of space was forever modified by the picture-making capacity of the camera.

A bird, then, can be fixed in time and space through a photograph (4.1). A highly realistic painting or drawing can come close to accomplishing the same thing. The artist is a necessary ingredient of this form. The drawings of Audubon, for example, were intended to be used as technical reference, and therefore are very realistic. Audubon studied and recorded the many varieties of birds of our country in astonishing and painstaking detail (4.2). We can say of his work: it is lifelike.

FIGURE 4.1   FIGURE 4.2

What we mean is the intention of the artist was to make the bird (or whatever is being visually reported on) look as much as possible as it looks naturally. Audubon was not only making a picture, he was also recording and supplying data for students that was dependable in identification, putting on paper visual information that could be used archivally for reference. In some ways, the photograph could be judged as more closely like life, but there is some argument that the artist's work is cleaner and clearer because he can control and manipulate it. This is the beginning of a process of abstraction, the removal of extraneous detail, the emphasis of distinguishing features.

The process of abstraction is one of distillation, the reduction of multiple visual factors to only the essential and most typical features of what is being represented. But if it is the movement of a bird that is to be emphasized, static and complete detail are ignored as in the sketch 4.3. In both cases of visual license, the final form follows the communication needs. In both cases, enough of the bird detail from life is present in the visual information to make the person who can recognize a bird able to recognize it in the sketches. Further deletion of detail toward total abstraction can take two paths: abstraction toward symbolism, sometimes with experienced meaning, sometimes with arbitrarily attached meaning, and pure abstraction, the reducing of the visual statement down to the basic elements, bearing no connection to any representational information drawn from experience of the environment.

FIGURE 4.3

SYMBOLISM

Abstraction toward symbolism requires ultimate simplicity, the reduction of visual detail to the irreducible minimum. A symbol, in order to be effective, must not only be seen and recognized but also remembered and even reproduced. It cannot, by definition, have a great deal of detailed information. It can, however, still retain some of the real qualities of a bird, as shown in Figure 4.4. In Figure 4.5, the same basic visual information of the bird shape with the addition of only

FIGURE 4.4   FIGURE 4.5

an olive branch, became the easily recognized symbol of peace. In this case, some education of the public may be necessary for the message to be clear. But the more abstract the symbol, the more penetration of the public mind is necessary for the education to its meaning. Figure 4.6 was once, in the symbolic gesture of World War II, the sign for the earnestly sought victory over the Germans in the war. It was frequently used by Winston Churchill, and was particularly taken up by the English following his lead. It was not unknown in the United States, and was often seen in photographs of GI's gesturing their hope of triumph from troopships, in the field, from hospital beds. It is truly ironic that this same gesture has been adopted by the anti-Vietnam war movement in the United States. For this movement, the gesture has come to mean peace. Another antiwar symbol of peace was first developed and used by the Nuclear Disarmament movement in England (4.7). Its visual derivation has been explained as the combination into one figure of the semaphore symbols for N and D.

Not only in language does the symbol exist as an information-packed means of visual communication, universal in meaning. It is used broadly. The symbol must be simple (4.8) and refer to a group, an idea, a business, an institution, or a political party. Sometimes it is abstracted from nature. It is even more effective for the transmission of information if it is a totally abstract figure (4.9). In this form it be-

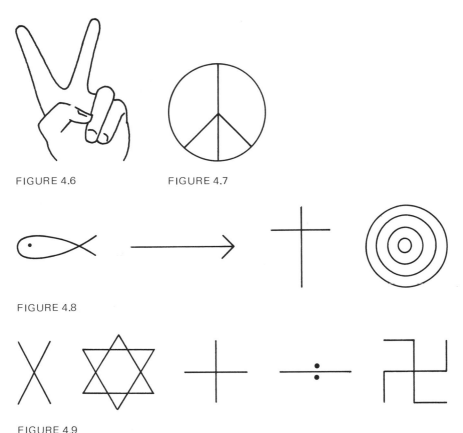

FIGURE 4.6   FIGURE 4.7

FIGURE 4.8

FIGURE 4.9

comes a code that serves as an adjunct to written language. The code
system of numbers provides examples of figures which are also abstract concepts.

1 2 3 4 5 6 7 8 9 0

There are many types of specialized coded information used by engi-
neers, architects, builders, electricians. One that many people learn
and communicate with is music (4.10). Each system has been developed to capsulize information so that it can be recorded and expressed to a mass audience.

Religion and folklore are rich in symbolism. The winged heel of Mer-
cury, Atlas holding the world on his shoulders, the witch's broom,
are just a few. Most familiar to us, as a visual language we all can nego-

FIGURE 4.10

ciate, is the symbolism of the holidays (4.11). Before our visual education, such as it was, stopped so suddenly after grammar school, all of us drew and colored these familiar symbols to decorate the classroom or to take along home. Large businesses, sensitive to their enormous propaganda effect, have moved strongly toward synthesizing their identities and purposes with visual symbols. It is a sound communication practice, for if, as the Chinese say, "One picture is worth a thousand words," then one symbol is worth a thousand pictures.

FIGURE 4.11

ABSTRACTION

Abstraction, however, need have no relationship to actual symbol-making when symbols have meaning only because it is pinned on them. The reduction of all we see to the basic visual elements is also a process of abstraction which, in fact, has far more significance to the understanding and structuring of visual messages. The more representational the visual information, the more specific its reference; the more abstract, the more general and all-encompassing it is. Abstraction, visually, is simplification toward a more intense and distilled meaning. As already demonstrated, human perception strips away surface detail in response to the need to establish balance and other visual rationalizations. But the importance to meaning does not end there. Abstraction can exist in visual matters not only in the purity of a visual statement stripped down to minimal representational information, but also as pure abstraction, which draws no connection with familiar visual data, environmental or experiential. The school of abstract painting is associated with the twentieth century, and includes the

work of Picasso, who has himself stretched his personal style from expressionistic to classical, to semi-abstract, to abstract (4.12). On the
one hand, he modified the visual facts to emphasize color and light,
but he retained the realistic, recognizable information. In another approach, an almost purist devotion to representational visual information, he echoed the godlike quality of man in only the slightly exaggerated realism of a classic style. His great liberties with reality resulted
first in highly maneuvered effects, and finally in the complete abandonment of the familiar for space and tone, color and texture. This
final visual style then was concerned only with the compositional
questions and content answers of design. In this evolution from
concern with observing and recording the world around to experimenting at the core of elemental visual message-making, Picasso followed a path of development that is not necessarily sequential, but
rather different stages of the same process. The path he followed may
be even more clearly observable in the work of J. M. W. Turner, who
as a young man pursued his craft almost like a reporter, using his
painting to detail and preserve his own time. But Turner became interested in the methods he used to develop a painting, particularly
in the sketch. Slowly his work evolved from a masterful representational technique to a loose and probing suggestion of reality, to, finally, almost totally abstract paintings with only the barest minimal visual clues of what he was picturing (4.13).

FIGURE 4.12 (continued on next page)

FIGURE 4.12 (continued)

FIGURE 4.13

The multiple levels of visual expression that include representationality, abstraction, and symbolism offer choices of both manner and
means to the solution to visual problems. Abstraction has been associated particularly with painting and sculpture as the unique pictorial
expression of the twentieth century. But many visual formats are by
their own nature abstract. A house, a dwelling, the simplest or most
complex shelter, does not look like anything drawn from nature. In
other words, a house is not patterned after a tree, which in some circumstances could be described as shelter; it looks like what it does;
its form follows its function. It is at its elemental level an abstract, dimensional volume. But the possible solutions for man's need for shelter and protection are infinite. They can be inspired by utility (4.14),
pride (4.15), expression (4.16), and communication and protection
(4.17). So the use that a building will be put to is one of the strongest
determining factors in its size, shape, proportion, tone, color, and texture. Form, in this case, as in other visual contexts, follows function.
But the where and when questions are also profoundly important to
the structural and style decisions that figure in the design and building of housing. The where is significant as to climate, since the requirements for shelter differ dramatically from the equator (4.18) to
the far North (4.19). Where something is being built also influences
the availability of materials. The branches and leaves of the tropics
are simply not available in the frozen reaches of the Arctic. Before it
is possible for form to follow the function, the form must be synthesized of a material or materials readily available in the environment.
Not just geographical location, but historical restraints, that is, when

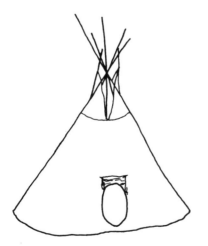

FIGURE 4.14   FIGURE 4.15

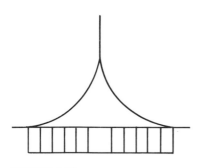

FIGURE 4.16

FIGURE 4.17

FIGURE 4.18

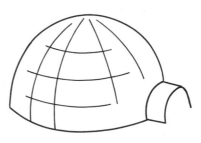

FIGURE 4.19

something is designed and built, often controls decisions of style and culture. For many of the above reasons, a particular design solution is arrived at and repeated with very little modification until it becomes identifiable in association with a certain period in time and a particular geographic location (4.18, 4.19). The last determining factor in this process is the idea and preference of the individual. Do not most people who have a hand in the designing and building of a house feel that it represents them? Even the fact of choice in the purchase of a house is considered a manifestation of their taste, and therefore, of them. How much visual information there is in all of this, and yet, consider, what we have been examining is the design and construction of buildings, all of which are abstract and possibly to some small extent, symbolic, but in no way representational. The meaning lies in the substructure, in the pure elemental visual forces, and because it lies within the province of the anatomy of a visual message, it is very intense communication.

It would appear to follow that any abstract visual statement is profound while the representational is, after all, just imitation and quite shallow in terms of depth of communication. But the fact is this: even as we view a highly representational, detailed, visual report of the environment, there coexists another visual message, exposing the elemental visual forces, abstract in quality (4.20, 4.21, 4.22), but packed with meaning, which has enormous power over response. The abstract understructure is the composition, the design. The potential for mes-

FIGURE 4.20

FIGURE 4.21

FIGURE 4.22

sage-making in the reduction of the realistic visual information to abstract components lies in the response of the arrangement to the effect intended. Can there be hard meaning in the abstract understructure? Music is, after all, totally abstract.... Yet, we characterize musical content as happy, sad, lively, turgid, martial, romantic. How do we arrive at such information identification, which is rather universally held? Some meanings attached to musical composition are associations to reality, some are drawn from man's own psychophysical structure, his kinesthetic relationship to the music. So we say of music: it is totally abstract, but there are aspects of it which may be interpreted with reference to shared meaning. In fact, the abstract quality may indeed increase the obtainability of the message and mood. In the visual formats, it is the composition which is the abstract counterpart of music, whether it is the visual statement itself or the understructure. The abstract conveys the essential meaning, cutting through the conscious to the unconscious, from the experience of the substance in the sensory field directly to the nervous system, from the event to perception.

INTERACTION AMONG THE THREE LEVELS
The levels of all visual stimuli contribute to the process of conceiving

and making and refining all visual work. To be visually literate, it is extremely necessary that the creator of the visual work be aware of each of these individual levels; but also it is important that the viewer or subject have equal awareness of them. Each level, representational, abstract, symbolic, has its own unique characteristics which can be isolated and defined, but they in no way conflict. In fact they overlap, interact, and enhance the individual qualities of each other.

The representational visual information is the most effective level to utilize in the strong, direct reporting of the visual details of the environment, both natural and made. Until the invention of the camera, only those highly talented and trained members of a community could produce the kinds of drawings and painting and sculpture that could successfully represent visual information as it appears to the eye. This facility has always been admired and the artist who could produce it has always been viewed as very special. There is a kind of magic in the very detailed and realistic visual work even though it might be regarded as surface or superficial. The comment about a portrait that "it looks just like me," has a very special recognition of the artist. But all this has changed with the camera. There is no question that, from a snapshot to the meticulously lit studio portrait, the problem of likeness doesn't even enter into the evaluation of a portrait. The camera delivers a visual report of whatever is in front of it with startling dependability and detail. It reports what it sees almost to a fault. But the visual communicator has many ways to control the results both in terms of style and technique. Nevertheless, representationality, the realistic report of what it sees, is natural to the camera and may well be one of the major factors in an increasing interest in the second level of visual information, the abstract.

Abstraction has, as already noted, been the primary tool in the development of a visual plan. It is most useful in the process of uncommitted exploration of a problem and development of visible options and solutions. The nature of abstraction releases the visualizer from the demands of representing the finished final solution, and so allows the underlying structural forces of the compositional questions to surface, the pure visual elements to appear, and the techniques to be applied with direct experimentation. It is a dynamic process filled with starts and false starts but free and easy by nature. It is not surprising that many artists are interested in the purity of the level. As noted above, the artist and visualizer may well have been released into a freer approach to visual expression by the natural mechanical prowess of the camera to reproduce a final, finished visual statement. Why compete? There always have been artists who have the training, the talent, and the interest to continue in the tradition of realism, from Salvador Dali and his hyper-realistic but subjectively interpreted surrealistic works to the subtly representational paintings of Andrew Wyeth. There, no doubt, always will be.

The interest in the free probes for visual solutions, however, is an unavoidable must for any artist or designer who must start from the blank sheet and work toward composing and completing a visual plan. This is not true for the photographer or filmmaker or television cameraman. In each case, the basic visual work is dominated by realistic information in detail, and therefore, inhibits the filmic thinker from investigation of the visual pre-plan. In film and television there is a component of language inherent in the planning process, but sad to say, words are frequently used in the previsualization of a film rather than visuals. A deeper awareness of the character of the abstract level of visual messages on the part of all those who use the lens can open up new avenues for visual expression of ideas.

The last level of visual information, the symbolic, has been commented on at great length. The symbol is anything from a simplified picture to a highly complex system of attached meaning like language or numbers. In all its formulations it can reinforce message and meaning in visual communication many ways. In print, it is a large and important component of the total character of a book, a magazine, or a poster, and must be dealt with in the forming of a design as abstract visual data, despite the fact that it is information with its own integrity and form. For the designer it is an interactive force which must be dealt with in terms of meaning and visual appearance.

The process of creating a visual message can be described as a series of steps from a number of rough sketches probing for solutions to increasingly refined versions toward a final choice and decision. It is necessary to add a proviso, namely: the word final describes any point the visualizer determines. The key to perception lies in the fact that the whole creative process seems to reverse for the receiver of visual messages. First, he sees the visual facts, either information drawn from the environment which can be recognized, or symbols which can be defined. On the second level of perception, the subject sees the compositional content, the basic elements, the techniques. It is an unconscious process, but through it is the cumulative experience of information input. If the original compositional intentions of the visual message-maker are successful, that is, have been brought to a sound solution, the result is coherent and clear, a working whole. If the solutions are extremely successful, the relationship between content and form can be described as elegant. With bad strategic decisions, the final visual effect is ambiguous. Aesthetic judgments involving words like "beauty" need not be involved at this level of interpretation, but rather left to a more subjective point of view. The interaction between purpose and composition, between syntactical structure and visual substance, must be mutually strengthening to be visually effective. Together, they represent the most important force in all visual communication, the anatomy of a visual message.

EXERCISES

1. Photograph or find an example of each of the three levels of visual material, Representational, Abstract, Symbolic.

2. Take a photograph out-of and in focus and study the abstract, out-of-focus version for its compositional feeling. Evaluate how you feel the abstract message relates to the representational statement. Could it be improved by changing the point of view of the camera? Make a rough sketch to see how you might change it by moving the camera.

3. Find a symbol which you can draw, and compare the ease with which you can reproduce it with the letters of the alphabet or numerals.

4. Divide up a photograph into even strips either horizontally or vertically and rearrange the order with some plan.

Any rearrangement will break down the representational order and reveal the abstract compositional structure.

5
THE DYNAMICS OF CONTRAST

The strongest control of visual effect lies in the understanding of the connection between message and meaning and the visual techniques. The syntactical guidelines offered by the psychology of perception, the familiarity with the character and appropriateness of the essential visual elements, provide those seeking visual literacy a firm foundation for compositional decisions. But the crucial control of visual meaning lies in the focusing function of the techniques. And of all the many visual techniques we will be investigating, none is more important to the control of a visual message than contrast.

CONTRAST AND HARMONY
Visual techniques, as already noted, have been arranged in polarities not only to demonstrate and accentuate the wide range of operative choices available in the design and interpretation of any visual statement, but, also, to express the intense importance of the technique and concept of contrast to the entire medium of visual expression.

All meaning exists in the context of polarities. Would there be understanding of hot without cold, high without low, sweet without sour? The contrast of substances and the sensorium's responsiveness to it dramatizes meaning through the opposite formulations. "The basic principle of 'form' determines that close relation between apperceptive unity and logical distinctions which was known to the ancients as 'unity in diversity.'" This is how Susanne Langer, in her essay, "Abstraction in Science and Abstraction in Art"* describes the "articulation of structural elements of a given whole." In the process of visual articulation, contrast is a vital force in creating a coherent whole. In all of art, contrast is a powerful tool of expression, the means for intensification of meaning and, therefore, of the simplification of communication.

Although on the list of techniques harmony is advanced as the polarity of contrast, it should be noted with great emphasis that the importance of both have a deeper significance in the entire visual process. They represent an ongoing and highly active process in how we see visual data and, consequently, how we understand what we see. The human organism seems to seek harmony, a state of ease, of resolution, what the Zen Buddhists speak of as "meditation in supreme repose." There is a need to organize all stimuli into rational wholes

*In Problems of Art

as demonstrated by the experiments of the Gestaltists. To reduce tension, to rationalize and explain, to resolve confusion, all appear dominant in man's needs. Only in the context of the logical conclusion of this endless and active quest does the value of contrast become clear. If the human mind got what it so fervently sought in all of its thought processes, what would it be? A state of weightless, fixed, motionless balance—absolute balance. Contrast is a counterforce to this human appetite. It unbalances, shocks, stimulates, arrests attention. Without it, the mind would move toward eradicating all sensation, creating a climate of death, of nonbeing. Whether or not we all feel a strong death wish, a nagging little voice in the ear of the trapeze artist whispering "let go," the state of absolute resolution, closure, is not final or finished or zero sensation enough. Like the all middle-gray environment, there would still be a sensation of sight without seeing, life without living. We would be like Palinurus, buried alive and cursed to sense all things from the grave, a living death. Psychologists tell us that our dreams are a kind of perspiration of the mind, throwing off the poisons of the psyche in a constant process of cleansing and clarification and absolutely essential to our mental health. So, also, the very process of living seems to demand a richness of sensory experience, especially through sight. We see so much more than we need to see, but our visual appetite is never satisfied. We reach out to the world and its complexities through our vision and we reach out through what the poets call "our mind's eye" to think visually. If, in its workings, the visual process moves toward absolute neutrality, it is the process and not the end result that should concern us.

THE ROLE OF CONTRAST IN SEEING

In visual literacy the importance of the meaning of contrast begins at the base level of seeing or not seeing at all through the presence or absence of light. No matter how well the physiological equipment of sight functions, the eyes, the nervous system, the brain, or how much there is in the environment to see, in a totally dark circumstance, we are all, in effect, blind. The human equipment for sight is of secondary importance; light is the key visual force. In its elemental visual state, light is tonal, reaching from brightness (or lightness) to darkness in a series of steps which can be described as having very subtle gradations. In the process of seeing, we are dependent on observing the interactive juxtaposition of those gradations of tone in order to see objects. Remember that the presence or absence of color does not affect tonal values; they are constant and hold infinitely more importance than color in seeing as well as designing and making. In pigment, lightness is synthesized or suggested by whiteness toward absolute white, while darkness is suggested by blackness toward absolute black. So everything we see can be invested with both properties of tonal values, the pigment quality of relative whiteness or blackness of tone and the physical quality of lightness or darkness. Physical light has a broad range of tonal intensity, while pigment is usually used in a limited range of eight to fourteen tonal steps. The broadest range of distinctly different gray tones in pigment is about thirty-five. Without light upon it, the whitest of whites will not be seen. So, whether from the sun or the moon or candlelight or the incandescence of the electric light bulb, light is the essential link in our physiological capacity of vision.

But the absence of light is not unique in its potential for blocking sight. If our entire environment were composed of an equal and matching value of a middle tone of gray, halfway between black and white, it would be possible to see; that is, we would not be experiencing the sensation of blindness created by a totally black environment. However, the ability to discern what we were seeing would be entirely erased from our perceptions. In other words, the contrast of tone is as vitally important as the presence of light in the process of seeing. Through tone, we can perceive patterns that we simplify into objects with shape, dimension, and other elemental visual properties. It is a decoding process of constant simplification of the raw data until, through it, we come to recognize and learn about the world we live in from the ants, moving about busily on the ground, to the stars, flickering with various sizes and tonal intensities in the sky. Light creates patterns, and once these patterns are identified, the information gained is stored in the brain to be utilized in recognition. It is an intricate and tricky process, described artfully by Bernard Berenson in his essay, Seeing and Knowing: "I see masses of green, opaque or translucent or glistening. They are spiky or smooth and, as if supporting them, roughly cylindrical somethings, vaguely brownish, greenish, grayish. I have learned in babyhood that they are trees and I vest them with trunks, with branches, with twigs, with foliage, with single leaves, according to their presumed species, ilex, chestnut, pine, olive, although my eyes see only varying shades of green."

So the eyes and the process of sight extend in many directions beyond seeing into the realm and workings of intelligence. The entire nervous system interacts with sight, enhancing our ability to discriminate. Touch, taste, hearing, smelling all contribute to our comprehension of the world around us, augmenting and, sometimes, contradicting what our eyes tell us. We touch something to determine if it is soft or hard; we smell something to discover if it is fragrant; we taste something to find if its pleasant odor indicates that it is equally pleasant to eat; and we listen to know if something is moving or still. All our senses are discriminating and constantly refining our recognition and understanding of the environment. But, of all our senses, there is little argument that the one we depend on the most, the one that has superior power, is sight. And sight functions most effectively when the patterns we observe are visually clarified through contrast. In nature and in art, contrast is of key importance to the visualizer in what Donald Anderson in his book, <u>Elements of Design</u>, calls "manipulating a set of such raw materials as clay, wire, pigment, data, sounds, words, numbers ... transforming them into cohesive structures on a higher level of significance."

THE ROLE OF CONTRAST IN COMPOSITION

Vision is intensely involved in pattern perception, a process that legislates toward a need for discernment. R. L. Gregory in <u>The Intelligent Eye</u> says: "In this sense 'patterns' are very different from 'objects.' By a pattern we mean some set of inputs, in space or time, at the receptor." Seeing means sorting out the patterns toward the end of understanding or recognition. Ambiguity is its natural enemy and must be avoided if the process of seeing is to function properly. We observe a tree. If it is upright and solid looking, we know we can lean on it. If it looks dangerously tipped and loose, we would not trust our weight to it. But if it is a little bit of both, not quite shaky, but on the other hand, not strong and upright either, then we are faced with confusing visual information. The pattern, the visual input, is inconclusive. Other methods of testing the sturdiness of the tree would have to be used. A line drawn through a square very close to dead center and yet off of it, is a more abstract example of the same con-

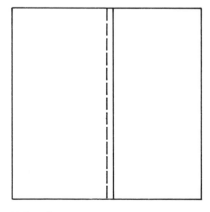

FIGURE 5.1

dition (5.1). The line is just enough off of the felt axis to disturb and upset the viewer, but not enough off to make its unbalanced position distinctly clear. The most effective utilization of the mechanisms of visual perception is to position or identify visual clues as one thing or the other, in balance or off, strong or threateningly weak. The Gestaltists deal with this need by describing the two opposite visual states as leveled or sharpened. Koffka, in his book, <u>Principles of Gestalt Psychology</u>, defines sharpening as "an increase or exaggeration" and leveling as "a weakening or toning down of a peculiarity of a pattern." In the terminology of visual techniques, sharpening can be equated with contrast (5.2), while leveling can be associated with harmony (5.3). But whatever descriptive language is used to describe the two polarities of visual composition, leveled or sharpened, the point must be emphasized that they are both excellent tools for constructing a visual statement with clarity of point of view. The use of them in a craftsmanlike manner goes a long way toward avoiding confusion for both the designer and his viewer.

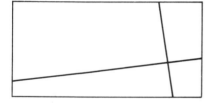

FIGURE 5.2

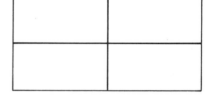

FIGURE 5.3

What the Gestaltists have researched and established through their recognition of the value of these two visual techniques is that the eye (and along with it, the human brain) will not be deterred in its endless pursuit of resolution or closure in the sensory data it views. Wertheimer introduced the principle which governs this hypothesis and called it "the law of Prägnanz," which he defines as follows: "psychological organization will always be as 'good' as the prevailing conditions allow." What is meant by "good" is not entirely clear. No doubt what he is suggesting is resolution in terms of regularity, symmetry, simplicity. Such forces as the need to finish off or connect an unfinished line (5.4) as in closure or to match like shapes as in the "principle of similarity" apply here (5.5). Finishing the lines or grouping the similar shapes is a step toward simplification, an inevitable step in the mechanics of perception in the human organism. But, is it as desirable as the physiological pull toward it would indicate? Absolute regularity can be refined and regulated toward a perfect end result in a visu-

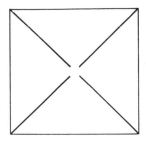

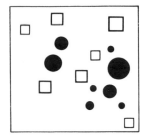

FIGURE 5.4   FIGURE 5.5

al statement. It is easy to determine and simple to respond to. Nothing is left to chance, or emotion, or subjective interpretation at either end of the stimulus ⟷ response communication model. The Greeks demonstrate the absolute and logical pursuit of harmonious results in the design of such temples as the Parthenon. Not only is there a utilization of the formula of the "Golden Mean," the mathematically determined proportion, but there is the most complete use of axial or symmetrical balance (5.6). Even tricks of perception are anticipated in the design and construction so that what is seen is as near perfect as man can achieve. Since the eye bends a straight line into a concave curve (5.7a) very slightly as it looks at it from a distance, the Greek architects designed the column of the temple facade with a slight—in fact, imperceptible—convexity (5.7b) to compensate for the phenomenon and to produce an apparently perfect straight line (5.7c). They would stop at nothing in their pursuit of perfection. The final effect was what they really sought, an effect that was completely har-

FIGURE 5.6

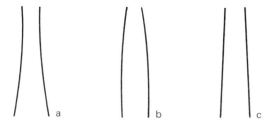

FIGURE 5.7

monious and balanced, in which nothing was left visually unresolved. We call the Greek style "classical," and associate with the quality of that style a total stability, with no equivocation on the part of the designer and no factors to unsettle the viewer. Certainly it all answers to the criteria that will produce the ideal of Wertheimer's "good" described in his "law of Prägnanz"; it conforms to the unconscious demands of the mind and the physical mechanics of the body. It is a quality that official institutions have certainly appropriated in the modern, Western world, and the classical style appears often in public buildings, particularly courthouses. Not only does the choice of architectural style associate its builders to the love of learning and the democratic ideals of the Greeks, but also to their rationality of balance. The blindfolded figure of Justice seeking balance and fairness, as shown symbolically in the scales she holds, is visually fulfilled in the symmetry of the design of a Greek temple.

But "good" as it is defined in the "law of Prägnanz" does not need symmetry and balance as its only expression; "good" in this sense also describes the clarity in a visual statement that can be produced through sharpening, or, as it can also be defined, the technique of contrast. Even though the obvious and most apparent need of the human being is for balance and repose, the need for resolution is equally strong, and sharpening offers great potential for achieving it, resolution that is an extension of the inner idea of harmony and is drawn from the organization of complexity rather than pure simplicity. Rudolf Arnheim in Art and Visual Perception calls the apparent contradiction in this fact "a duality connected to the parallel activities of the process of growth and the striving for vital aims." Leveling (5.8), as in the design of the facade of a Greek temple, is harmonious and simple, but sharpening (5.9) has much more vital intentions in its visual character. And yet it would be unfair to say that one was easier to perceive than the other. They are merely different.

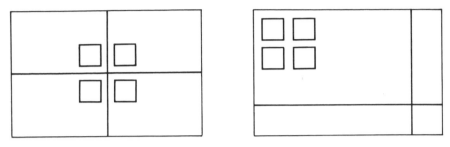

FIGURE 5.8   FIGURE 5.9

The act of seeing is a process of discernment and judgment. In Figure
5.8, both processes can be activated and the results of their workings
can be established quickly and automatically by the viewer. The example demonstrates complete and indisputable balance. But the same
quick and automatic response on the part of the viewer to Figure 5.9
can be predicted. The definition of the structure is not as unequivocal
except in a negative sense; the visual elements are not symmetrical. It
does not balance in the obvious sense that the elements in Figure 5.8
do. But balance does not have to take the form of symmetry. The
weight of the design elements can be adjusted asymmetrically. The
additional forces move the design away from simplicity, but the final
effect is one of balance structured by weight and counterweight, action and counteraction. The final effect can be read and responded to
quite clearly by the viewer; it is just a more complex process and
therefore slower (5.10). The same psychophysiological human perceptual ability that establishes symmetrical balance can automatically
measure and respond to asymmetrical balance. The process is not as
easily demonstrated and defined, and, consequently, often seems intuitive rather than physical.

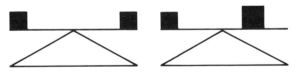

FIGURE 5.10

One thing is certain about the asymmetrical balance of Figure 5.10,
and that is that it is not almost balanced symmetrically. The viewer
is not provoked by lack of resolution or upset with visual ambiguity.
The design is clearly nonaxial balance, and because of the clarity of
this fact we can say it is a good demonstration of the state of visual

"sharpening." To make a clear visual statement, the choice must go clearly one way or the other, leveled or sharpened, contrasted or harmonious. The designer must be enjoined to follow the dictum of the Yankee fisherman to "fish or cut bait." The area between the polarities of leveling and sharpening is murky and unclear, and should usually be avoided as bad communication and as aesthetically ugly. When the visual intentions of the designer are not strongly delineated and controlled, the result is ambiguous and the effect created is an unsatisfying and frustrating one for the audience (5.11). The balance cannot be established clearly one way or the other; the elements cannot be organized and related, primarily to one another, and, secondarily, to the field. Unless that is the visual impression that is sought by the designer (an unlikely possibility), ambiguity should be avoided as the most undesirable visual effect, not just because it is psychologically upsetting, but because it is sloppy and inferior on any level of the criteria of visual communication.

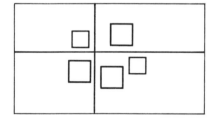

FIGURE 5.11

Harmony, or the leveled state in visual design, is a useful and almost foolproof method for the solution of compositional problems for the inexperienced and unskilled visual message-maker. The rules to follow are as simple and clear as can be, and if they are followed rigidly, the results are predictably attractive. You just cannot go wrong. For reasons of insurance and assurance, axial balance as a design strategy has been an invaluable aid in the constructing of clean, neat designs. Book design has been dominated by the classical look of pages in absolute balance (5.12), especially since the invention of metal movable type. The mechanical, mathematical nature of typesetting lends itself perfectly to formula computations that produce balance. But, as safe and sure as the harmonious technique offered by leveled design may be in providing, as it does in book design, a nonintrusive visual setting for the message, the mind and the eye demand stimulation. Boredom is as much a threat in visual design as it is elsewhere in art and com-

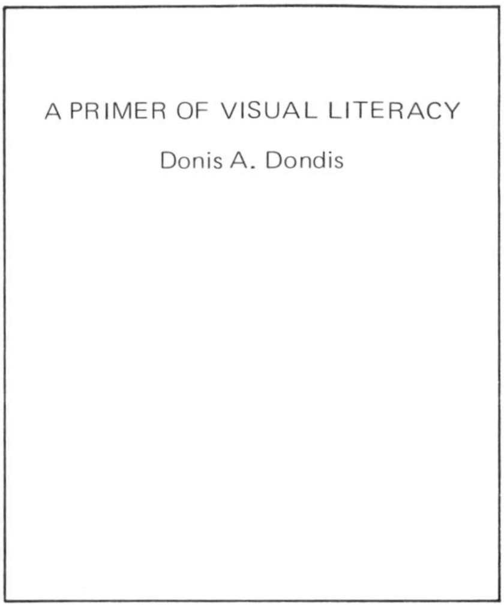

A PRIMER OF VISUAL LITERACY

Donis A. Dondis

FIGURE 5.12

munication. The mind and the eye demand stimulation and surprise, and an approach to design that functions boldly and successfully suggests the need for sharpening of the structure and message.

As a visual strategy to sharpen meaning, contrast not only can excite and attract the attention of the viewer, but it can also dramatize that meaning to make it more important, more dynamic. If, for instance, you want something to look clearly large, put something small next to it. This is contrast, an organization of the visual stimuli toward an intense effect. But intensification of meaning goes even further than juxtaposition of unlike elements. It consists of a deletion of the superficial and unnecessary, which leads to a natural spotlighting of the essential. Rembrandt followed this method in the development of his technique of "chiaroscuro." The name of the technique is drawn from the combination of two Italian words: chiaro, which means light, and scuro, for dark. That is what he uses, lightness and darkness. In his paintings (5.13) and in his etchings (5.14), Rembrandt discarded the middle tones to accent and highlight his subject matter with a striking, theatrical look. The incredible richness of result is as strong an argument for the understanding and utilization of contrast as can be found in the body of visual work at any level.

Contrast is an essential tool in the strategy of control of visual effects and, consequently, meaning. But contrast is simultaneously a tool, a technique, and a concept. In basic terms, we have a deeper under-

FIGURE 5.13

FIGURE 5.14

standing of smooth if we juxtapose it to rough. It is a physical fact
that if you touch something rough and grainy, and then touch something smooth, the smooth will seem smoother. Opposites seem more
intensely themselves when you think of them in terms of their uniqueness. In this observation lies the essential meaning of the word contrast: to stand against. By comparing the unlike, we sharpen the
meaning of both. Contrast is a vital pathway to clarity of content in
art and communication. Susanne Langer, in her essay, "The Dynamic
Image,"* says of this phenomenon: "A work of art is a composition of
tensions and resolutions, balance and unbalance, rhythmic coherence,
a precarious yet continuous unity. Life is a natural process of such
tensions, balances, rhythms; it is these that we feel, in quietness or
emotion, as the pulse of our own living." But the pull demonstrated
by contrast between opposites must be handled as delicately as spice
in cooking. The main purpose of a visual statement is expression, the
conveying of ideas, information, and feelings; it must be seen in terms
of expression to be understood most easily. Rudolf Arnheim has giv-
en the most creative interpretation to the interaction of thought and
visual stimuli. In his essay, "Expression and Gestalt Theory," included in a broad collection of writings called Psychology and the Visual
Arts, Arnheim defines expression as the "psychological counterpart
of the dynamic processes which result in the organization of perceptual stimuli." In other words, the very same means the human organism uses to decode and organize and make sense out of visual information, all information for that matter, could serve most effectively
for composing a message to be viewed by an audience. The process of
human informational input, in its psychological and physiological
ramifications, could serve as a model for informational output.

Whether at the level of expression that involves only the contrast of
visual elements, or at the level of expression that involves conveying
complex visual information, a visual communicator must recognize
the efficient character of contrast, and its importance as a working
tool that can be used and should be used in visual composition. Contrast is the sharpener of all meaning; it is the basic definer of ideas.
There is so much richer an understanding of happiness when it is
thought of juxtaposed with sadness; love with hate; affection with
hostility; motivation with passivity; involvement with loneliness.
Each purely conceptual polarity can be associated with and expressed by visual elements and techniques that can be associated with

*In Problems of Art.

their meaning. Love, for instance, would be suggested by curves, circular shapes, warm colors, soft texture, similar proportions (5.15). Hate, as its polarity, would be reinforced by angles, straight shapes, hot colors, rough texture, dissimilar proportions (5.16). The elements are not absolutely opposite, but almost. Of all the visual techniques, it is contrast that is omnipresent in effective visual statements at all levels of the comprehensive structure of the message, conceptual and elemental. So it should be noted that contrast as an invaluable visual tool must constantly be referred to, from the generalized stage in visual composition right down to the specific character of each visual element chosen to articulate and express ideas visually.

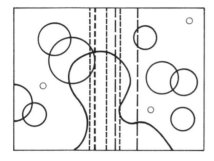

FIGURE 5.15

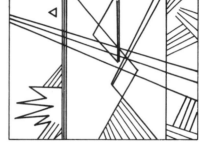

FIGURE 5.16

It is obviously more efficient to explain high by contrasting it with low, particularly in the use of visual stimuli (5.17). Proportion is vitally important in the manipulation of the field compositionally. To express precisely the emphasis of dissimilarity of visual clues, there-

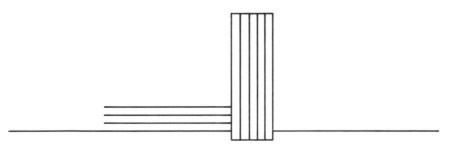

FIGURE 5.17

fore, the major point should have the largest proportion of space devoted to its display (5.18), at the least a two-thirds to one-third divi-

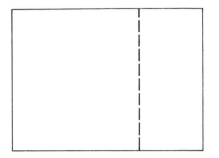

FIGURE 5.18

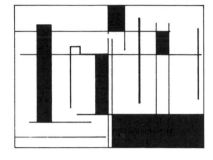

FIGURE 5.19

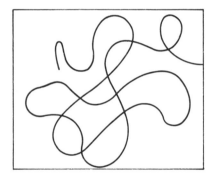

FIGURE 5.20

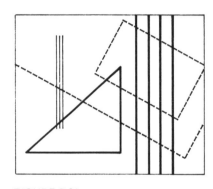

FIGURE 5.21

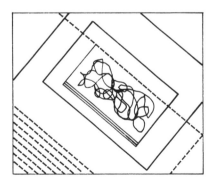

FIGURE 5.22

sion. This proportional division should increase the preciseness of intention in the composition (5.19). Whatever the effect intended, the
the primary information should have a disproportionate, large area of
the field devoted to it. Proportion and scale depend on manipulation
of size or space for effect, but, while this is a basic consideration in

the structure of contrast, it is not aboslutely necessary. Other elemental forces count for a great deal in the final effect. Each visual element offers multiple possibilities in the producing of contrasting visual information. Line, for instance, can be formal or informal, and
each carries strong informational clues. The looseness of informal
line creates a feeling of investigation and unresolved probing (5.20),
while the formal use of line connotes precision, plan, technics (5.21).
Only in the juxtaposition of the two opposites can we create a contrasting composition (5.22) in which the basic character of each line
treatment is accentuated.

CONTRAST IN TONE
With tone, the relative lightness or darkness in a field establishes the
intensity of contrast. Size or proportion is not the only consideration.
An equal division of a field can still demonstrate the contrast of tone
(5.23), since the heavier weight of black dominates the field. If an increasingly lighter tone were used in place of the black, the proportion

FIGURE 5.23

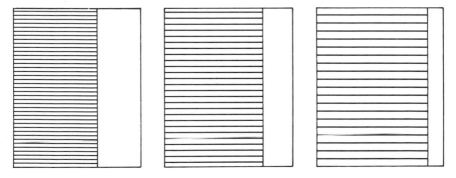

FIGURE 5.24

of the area covered by the deeper tone would have to be increased in order to sustain the effect of dominance and recessiveness that offers visual reinforcement to conceptual messages (5.24). Of course, tone is not usually distributed in a field in this regular and rigid way, and, yet, analysis of a visual composition can show whether there is a substantial enough division of tonal extremes toward an end of expressing contrast. Rembrandt went to great extremes to control his composition by using intense contrast, light against dark, dark against light, for the most compelling visual results in history.

CONTRAST IN COLOR
Tone supersedes color in our negotiation of the environment, and, therefore, tone has far more importance than color in the establishment of contrast. Of the three dimensions of color (hue, tone, chroma), it is the tone that dominates. Johannes Itten established a structural approach to the study and use of color based on many contrasts, primarily emphasizing the light-dark opposition. Probably the most important contrast in color, beyond the tonal, is the cold-warm contrast, which divides the red-yellow dominated warm colors from the blue-green, cool colors. The quality of recessiveness in the blue-green range has been used to indicate distance, while the dominant quality of the red-yellow range has been used to express expansiveness. These qualities can affect spatial position since the color temperature can suggest proximity and distance. Itten cites some other color contrasts, among them, complementary and simultaneous. Each deals with the quality of color that can be used to sharpen a visual statement. Complementary contrast in color is the relative balance of cool and warm. According to the Munsell theory of color, the complementary is the exact opposite on the color wheel. In pigment form, the complementaries demonstrate two things: first, when mixed together, they produce a neutral, median tone of gray; second, when juxtaposed, complementary colors provoke a maximum intensity from each other. Both actions are related to Munsell's theory of simultaneous contrast. Munsell established the opposite colors on the color wheel through the human physiological phenomenon of afterimage, that is the color you see on a blank white surface after you stare at any color for some seconds. The process takes yet another form. When a gray square is placed within the surface of a cool color, it will be seen as warm, that is, tinged with the complementary tone of the color it is placed within. In other words, the opposite color is not just experienced perceptually as an afterimage, but simultaneously in a physiological process of neutralization that relates to the apparent pull to-

ward reduction of all visual stimuli to the most neutral and simplified form possible. We feed the complementary color into whatever color we are viewing. So, it would appear, not only are we experiencing a constant stimulus reducing effect in our pattern perception, but also, we are physiologically engaged in a color erasing process in our visual informational input in a never-ending pursuit of a middle tone of gray. Contrast is the key antidote to this action.

CONTRAST IN SHAPE

The need of the whole system of human perception for leveling, for absolute balance, for visual closure, is the action against which contrast sets up a counteraction. In each instance of citing a basic visual element, we can quickly demonstrate the dynamics of contrast by constructing a compositional counterforce. Regular shape, simple and resolved, is dominated by the irregular, the unpredictable, in terms of attracting the attention of the viewer (5.25). Dissimilar textures intensify the unique quality of the other when they are juxtaposed (5.26). The same factors, of disproportionate and differentiated qualities juxtaposed, figure in the use of all the visual elements for the purpose of taking advantage of the value of contrast in the definition of visual meaning. The major function of the technique is sharpening through dramatic effect, but at the same time, it very successfully can refine the entire mood and sensation of a visual statement. Contrast must augment the designer's intentions.

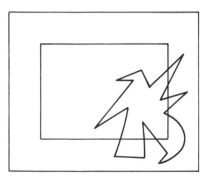

FIGURE 5.25

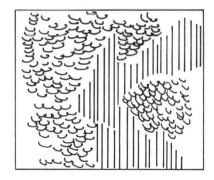

FIGURE 5.26

CONTRAST IN SCALE

Distortion of scale, for instance, can shock the eye by forcefully manipulating the proportion of objects and contradicting what experience has led us to expect to see (5.27). The idea or message underly-

FIGURE 5.27   FIGURE 5.28

FIGURE 5.29

ing the use of contrast through distorted scale should be logical; there
should be a rational reason for the manipulation of familiar visual objects. In this instance, the relationship between the meaning of the
large acorn in the foreground and the smaller oak tree in the background, reverses the "great oaks from little acorns grow" idea visually, yet it dramatizes the importance of the acorn and, by doing so, articulates the basic meaning intended. As a visual technique, contrast
can be further emphasized by juxtaposing different media. If the
acorn is rendered in tone and the tree in line (5.28) or the tonal rendition is a photograph and the line drawing is looser and more interpretive (5.29), the contrast is increased through elemental visual cues
from which we discern meaning.

Contrast, at the basic construction and decoding level, can be utilized through all the basic elements: line, tone, color, direction, shape, movement, and most particularly, proportion and scale. All are valuable forces in the ordering of visual input and output, emphasizing the key importance of contrast in the control of meaning. Any visual message combines the elements in a complex interaction. Many things are happening at once, and it is difficult to avoid confusion and ambiguity. If the final effect is to be coherent, the vague and the generalized must be modified by contrast toward the precise and the specific state of the concrete in a decision-making process of design. Seeing moves toward organization of data, reaching from the primary sensations, the expression and comprehension of simple ideas through increasing complexity to the abstract. Visual information has the same evolving character, but at any point in the hierarchy, it must be disciplined by the designer's intention to communicate. Whether in the case of an arrow cut into a tree to mark a pathway through the woods, or an imposing cathedral reaching its towers toward the sky, the organization of visual elements must respond to the purpose of the visual statement, the form must follow the function. In this pursuit, contrast is the bridge between the defining and comprehension of visual ideas, not in the verbal sense of definition, but in the visual sense of making ideas and sensations and images more visible.

EXERCISES
1. Make a photograph or find examples of both (1) a balanced, harmonious and (2) an asymmetrical, contrasting visual statement. Analyze and compare the effect of each and their ability to convey information or mood.

2. Choose two opposite conceptual ideas (love-hate, war-peace, city-country, organized-confused). In a square make a collage which represents the contrast of ideas by using visual techniques to reinforce the meaning through the visuals used.

3. Make a collage or photograph in which unlike visual materials are juxtaposed toward a heightened or sharpened effect of the message.

4. Look for an example of design or graphics where surprise in the juxtaposition of unexpected visual information dramatizes the artist's underlying intention.

6

VISUAL TECHNIQUES:
THE COMMUNICATION STRATEGIES

Content and form are the irreducible, basic components of all media, music, poetry, prose, the dance, and, as is our main concern here, the visual arts and crafts. Content is primarily what is being expressed, directly or obliquely; it is the character of the information, the message. But in visual communication, content is never detached from form. It changes subtly from medium to medium and format to format, adapting to the circumstances of each; from the design of a poster or newspaper or any other print format with its unique dependence on words and symbols, to a photograph with its characteristic realistic observations of environmental data, to an abstract painting with its utilization of pure visual elements in a skeleton structure. In each of these examples and many, many others the content may be basically the same, but it must respond to its setting, and in responding, make minor modifications in its elemental and compositional character. A message is composed with purpose: to tell, express, explain, direct, inspire, affect. In pursuit of any purpose, choices are made, choices meant to reinforce and strengthen expressive intentions for maximum control of response. This requires enormous skill. Composition is the interpretive means for controlling the reinterpretation of a visual message by those who experience it. Meaning lies as much in the eye of the beholder as in the talents of the creator. The end result of all visual experience, in nature but primarily in design, lies in the interaction of duplex polarities: first, the forces of content (message and meaning) and form (design, medium, and arrangement); and second, the effect on each other of the articulator (designer, artist, craftsman) and the receiver (audience) (6.1). In either case, one cannot be separated from the other. Form is affected by content; content is affected by form. The message is cast by the creator and modified by the observer.

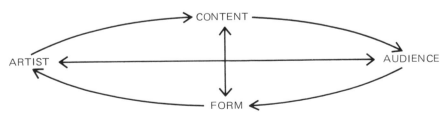

FIGURE 6.1

Symbols and representational information are weighted toward content as characteristic conveyers of information. Abstract design, the arrangement of the basic elements for an intended emotional effect in a visual statement, is the form revealed. The components of the form, that is, the composition, are concurrent or parallel aspects of every image, whether the structure is apparent, as in an abstract visual statement, or superseded by representational detail in realistic visual information, or dominated informationally by words and symbols. Whatever the basic visual substance, the composition is all-important informationally. This evaluation is supported by Susanne Langer in Problems of Art: "A picture is made by deploying pigments on a piece of canvas, but the picture is not a pigment and canvas structure. The picture that emerges from the process is a structure of space and the space itself is an emergent whole of shapes, visible colored volumes." Not in the physical substance but in the composition lies the message and meaning. The form expresses the content. "What is artistically good is whatever articulates and presents feeling to our understanding."

THE MESSAGE AND THE METHOD

The message and the method of expressing it depend heavily on the understanding and ability to use visual techniques, the tools of visual composition. In Elements of Design, Donald Anderson notes: "Technique is sometimes the fundamental force in abstraction, the reduction and simplification of complex and wandering detail to graphic relationships which can be grasped—to the form of art." Dominated by contrast, the techniques of visual expression are the essential means for the designer to probe the options available for expressing an idea compositionally. The process is one of experimentation and tentative selection toward an end of achieving the strongest visual solution possible for the expression of content. What happens is described by Leo Steinberg in his essay, "The Eye is Part of the Mind"*: "To bring his organizing powers into the fullest play, the painter must haul his perceptions out of their limbo and annex them to his plan." Not just in painting, but in every level of visual expression the problem is the same. Basically, pictorial or visual is determined by the visual information observed, the interpretation and perception of visual clues and data, the total visual statement. The designer-determined content and form represents only three of the four factors in the model of the visual communication process (6.1), artist, content,

*In Reflections on Art, Susanne K. Langer (ed.).

form. What of the fourth, the audience? Perception, the power to organize the visual information seen, depends on the natural workings, the needs and propensities of the human nervous system. While the whole body of work of the Gestalt school of psychology is called by the French, "la psychologie de la forme," it would be wrong not to give equal importance to the physiology of perception in the examination of how we retrieve visual information from what we see. The content and form is the statement; the mechanics of perception is the means for interpretation. Visual input is heavily affected by what needs motivate visual investigation and also by the state of mind or mood of the subject. We see what we need to see. Vision is linked to survival as its primary function. But we see what we need to see in another sense, that is, through the influence of mental set, preferences, and mood at any given moment. Whether in composing or viewing, the information in visual data must emerge from or be filtered by the net of subjective interpretation. "The words of a dead man are modified in the guts of the living," reflects W. H. Auden in his poem "In Memory of W. B. Yeats." In order to truly control effect as much as possible, the visual composer must understand the complex ways the human organism sees, and, through this knowledge, learn to influence response through the visual techniques.

Intelligence does not operate in verbal abstractions alone. Thinking, observing, understanding, so many of the qualities of intelligence, are linked to visual understanding. But visual thinking is not a delayed system; information is conveyed directly. The greatest power of visual language lies in its immediacy, its spontaneous evidence. Visually, you see content and form simultaneously. They must be dealt with as one single force delivering information the same way. Darkness is darkness; high is high; meaning is observable. Properly developed and composed, a visual message is channeled directly to our brain to be understood without conscious decoding, translating, or delay. "What you see is what you get," is the trademark comment of the comedian, Flip Wilson. How apt in terms of analysis of visual communication his quip is. In fact, it in no way conflicts with the observation of the great philosopher of aesthetics, Susanne Langer: "...as one psychologist who is also a musician has written, 'Music sounds as feelings feel.' And likewise in good painting, sculpture, or building, balanced shapes and colors, lines and masses look as emotions, vital tensions and their resolutions feel."* What you see, you see. Directness is the incompar-

*In Reflections on Art, Susanne K. Langer (ed.).

able power of visual intelligence. Recognition of this fact and potential reveals the key importance to control of that very special directness of expression unique in visual communication through the use of techniques which control the meaning in structure. Design, the manipulation of visual elements, is a fluid business, but the method of previsualization, of planning, illustrates the character of the synthesized message. It is a special kind of intelligence, nonverbal, and its quality is linked to the casting of content into form through the control exerted by technique. Again, Susanne Langer in Problems of Art describes the fact of visual expression so insightfully: "Form, in the sense in which artists speak of 'significant form' or 'expressive form' is not an abstracted structure, but an apparition; and the vital processes of sense and emotion that a good work of art expresses seem to the beholder to be directly contained in it, not symbolized but really presented. The congruence is so striking that symbol and meaning appear as one reality."

VISUAL INTELLIGENCE APPLIED
Previsualization is a loose process. Ideally, it is the stage of design when the artist-composer manipulates the pertinent visual element with techniques appropriate to content and message in a free-wheeling series of tryouts. Detail, maybe even recognizable connections with the end result, are abandoned as unnecessary in this period of development of a visual idea. Each artist develops a shorthand of his own. Probably because of the looseness and casualness of this step in seeking a compositional solution that pleases the designer, serves the function, and expresses the ideas or character desired, the making of visual statement has been associated with noncerebration. A series of rough, ostensibly undisciplined sketches certainly does not suggest intellectual rigor. The artist, after all, is considered to be in a kind of mesmerized state, "flying by the seat of his pants" as he makes decisions. What is really going on? The reality is that the artist, designer, craftsman, the visual communicator is engaged at this crucial point of decision in a highly complex process of selection and rejection.

Talent, artistic control of medium, and intuition have become somewhat confused. In fact, what we call intuition in art is extremely misleading. While the root of the word in Latin, intuitus, means "to look at or contemplate," the English usage has come to indicate a special kind of knowing, "knowledge or cognition without rational thought." The dictionary definition also lists such descriptions of meaning as "immediate apprehension or cognition" and "quick and ready insight." The combination adds to the confusion. Immediate apprehension of meaning in visual matters makes it all seem too easy to be taken seriously intellectually. And the artist is unjustly stripped of his special genius.

Any visual venture, no matter how simple, basic, or lowly, involves making something that was not there before, making palpable that which does not yet exist. But anyone can make or design something, even if it is only a mudpie. There are criteria to be applied to the process and to our judgment of it. Sudden inspiration, mindlessness, is not an acceptable force in design. Careful planning, intellectual probing, technical knowledge are necessities in visual pre-planning and design. The artist must seek through his compositional strategies solutions to questions of beauty and functionality, of balance and the mutual support of form and content. His quest is highly intellectual; his options through choice of techniques must be cerebral and in control. Creating in the visual mode at multiple levels of function and expression cannot be accomplished in a semi-comatose aesthetic state, no matter how blessed it allegedly is. Visual intelligence is no different than general intelligence and the control of the elements of visual media presents the same problems as the mastery of any skill. To accomplish it, you must know what you are working with and how to proceed.

Visual composition starts with the basic elements: dot, line, shape, direction, texture, dimension, scale, and movement. The first step in composition is based on a choice of elements appropriate to the medium to be dealt with. In other words, form is the elemental structure. But what to do in the making of the elemental structure? The options and choices that lead to expressive effect depend on the manipulation of the elements by visual techniques. Between the two, elements and techniques, and the multiple means they offer the designer, there are truly limitless choices for control of content. The literally infinite options of design make it difficult to describe the visual techniques in the rigidly definitive way we establish common meaning in words.

Seeing is a natural fact for the human organism; perception is an enabling process. Designing has to do with a little bit of both. To hear does not imply the ability to write music, and, by the same token, to see does not in any way guarantee the ability to make understandable, functional visual statements. Intuition is simply not enough; it is not a mystical force in visual expression. Visual meaning as conveyed by composition, by manipulation of elements, by visual techniques involves a galaxy of specific factors and forces. The primary technique is, without question, contrast. This is the force that makes the compositional strategies more visible. But meaning emerges from the psychophysiological actions of outside stimuli on the human organism: the tendency to organize all visual cues into the simplest forms possible; the automatic relating of visual cues with identifiable similarities; the overriding need for balance; the compelling connection of visual units born of proximity; the favoring of left-over-right and the lower over the upper areas of a viewing field. These are all factors that monitor visual perception, and to recognize how they operate can enhance or negate the use of technique. Beyond operative knowledge of these and other human perceptual phenomena lies the form of all things visual in art, in manufacture, in nature. The character and perception of it creates the whole, the form. Paul Stern deals with the definition in his essay, "On the Problems of Artistic Form"*: "It is only when all the factors of an image, all their individual effects are completely attuned to the one intrinsic vital feeling that is expressed in the whole—when, so to speak, the clarity of the image coincides with the clarity of the inner content—that a truly artistic 'form' is achieved." Form, in its visual manifestation, is composed of the elements and their character and arrangement, and the energy they provoke in the viewer. The choice of which of the basic elements are employed in a design and how they are used has to do with both form and the direction of energy released by the form which results in content. The analyzed and stated objective of the visual composer, whether informational, or functional, or both, serves as a guideline for seeking the form a visual statement will take. If, as Louis Sullivan has proclaimed, "form follows function," then it would be a logical extension of his thinking to add, "form follows content." An airplane looks like what it does. Its form is governed and shaped by what it does. A poster for a church fair in summer should do the same. It should be shaped not so much by function in a mechanistic sense, but by function of content. Does it express the purpose for which it was made? It should be bright and gay and engaging and busy and amusing. It should represent and reveal its purpose. Not just through words or symbols but through the total composition. It would be quite within the creative options of a designer to compose a formal and unreadable poster for the purpose outlined (6.2), but the results would have little to do with what the poster was for. One can observe that the choices of techniques are ineffectual. What visual techniques can express the es-

*In Reflections on Art, Susanne K. Langer (ed.).

COME TO THE FAIR
GAMES   EXHIBITS
FUN, RIDES, PRIZES
DON'T MISS IT!
SATURDAY

FIGURE 6.2   FIGURE 6.3

sence of the event through a poster? Brightness of tone and fragmentation suggest excitement; spontaneity indicates involvement and movement. Clear display of the verbal message responds to the function of the poster, namely, to solicit attendance. Put them all together and you arrive at one solution (6.3) which seems appropriate.

TECHNIQUES FOR VISUAL COMMUNICATION

The visual techniques offer the designer a wide palette of means for the visual expression of content. They exist as polarities on a continuum, or as unlike and opposite approaches to meaning. Fragmentation, the opposite of the technique of unity, is an excellent choice for the expression of excitement and variety as demonstrated in Figure 6.3. How would it function as the compositional strategy for the reflection of the character of a hospital? Analysis of that character and a plan to represent it compositionally would follow the same pattern for seeking effective verbal descriptions. Clearly, "fragmentation" is a bad choice of technique to associate with a medical center, but quite apt for the reinforcement of the announcement of a church fair. The inner meaning of both legislates the choices the designer has for representing them. Those choices represent the control of effect that ends in strong composition.

Visual techniques do not have to be thought of as either/or choices for constructing or analyzing anything that will be seen. The extremes of meaning can be modified to lesser degrees of intensity like the step tones of gray between black and white. In these variations lies a highly expanded range of possibilities for expression and understanding. The subtleties of composition available to the designer are in part due to the multiple options, but also, visual techniques are combined and interactive in their compositional use. One point should be clarified and that is that the polarities of techniques should never be so subtle as to be unclear. While they do not need to be utilized only in their intense extremes, they should be clearly one way or the other. If they are not definable, they become ambiguous, bad conveyers of information. The danger is especially serious in visual communication, which operates with such speed and directness as an information channel.

It would be impossible to name all the visual techniques available, or, in naming them, succeed in giving them hard definitions. Here, as it obtains in every step of the structure of the visual means, personal interpretation is an important factor. But operating within those limitations, each technique and its opposite can be defined as a polarity.

BALANCE   INSTABILITY
Second in importance to contrast in the visual techniques is balance (6.4). Its primary importance is based on the operation of human perception and the intense need for it in both designing and reacting to a visual statement. Its opposite on a polar continuum is instability. Balance is a design strategy in which there is a center of suspension midway between two weights. Instability (6.5) is the absence of balance and a highly upsetting and provoking visual formulation.

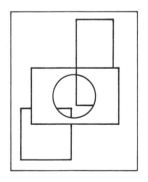  

FIGURE 6.4. BALANCE

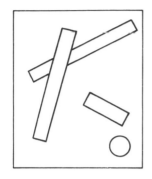

FIGURE 6.5. INSTABILITY

SYMMETRY   ASYMMETRY

Balance can be achieved in a visual statement two ways, symmetrically (6.6) and asymmetrically (6.7). Symmetry is axial balance. It is a
totally resolved visual formulation in which every unit on one side of

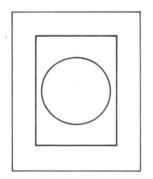

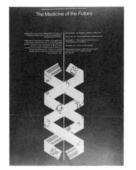

FIGURE 6.6. SYMMETRY

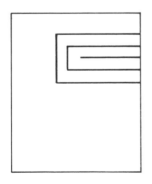

FIGURE 6.7. ASYMMETRY

a center line is replicated exactly on the other side. It is completely logical and simple to design, but can be static and even boring. Asymmetry would be considered ill-balanced by the Greeks, but, in fact, balance can be achieved by variation in elements and placement, which is a counterpoise of weights. The visual equilibrium in such a design is complicated by adjustment of many forces, but is interesting and rich in its variety.

REGULARITY   IRREGULARITY

Regularity (6.8) in design is the favoring of uniformity of elements, the development of an order based on some principle or method that is undeviating. Its opposite is irregularity (6.9), which, as a design strategy, emphasizes the unexpected and unusual, not conforming to any decipherable plan.

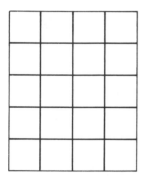

FIGURE 6.8. REGULARITY

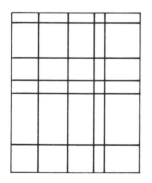

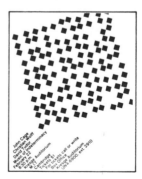

FIGURE 6.9. IRREGULARITY

SIMPLICITY   COMPLEXITY

Order contributes a great deal to the visual synthesis of simplicity

(6.10), a visual technique of directness and singleness of elemental form, free from secondary complications or elaboration. Its opposite visual formulation, complexity (6.11), comprises a visual intricacy made up of many elemental units and forces and results in a difficult process of organizing the meaning in the pattern.

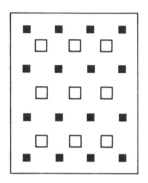

FIGURE 6.10. SIMPLICITY

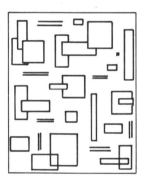

FIGURE 6.11. COMPLEXITY

UNITY   FRAGMENTATION

The techniques of unity (6.12) and fragmentation (6.13) are similar to and involved with the same design strategies as simplicity-complexity. Unity is a proper balance of diverse elements into one totality that is visually all of a piece. The collection of many units should dovetail so completely that it is viewed and considered as a single thing. Fragmentation is the breaking up of the elements and units of a design into separate pieces that relate but retain their own individual character.

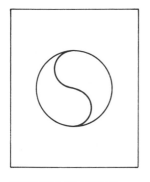

FIGURE 6.12. UNITY

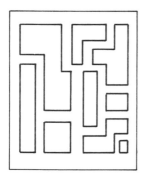

FIGURE 6.13. FRAGMENTATION

ECONOMY   INTRICACY

The presence of minimum units of visual means is typical of the tech-

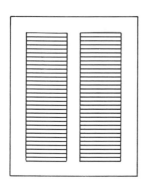

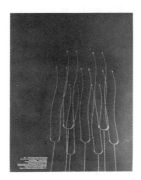

FIGURE 6.14. ECONOMY

FIGURE 6.15. INTRICACY

nique of economy (6.14) which contrasts with its polar technique of
intricacy (6.15) in many ways. Economy is a visual arrangement that
is frugal and judicious in the utilization of elements. Intricacy is
heavily weighted toward a technique of endlessly detailed discursive
additions to a basic design that, ideally, soften and make more beautiful through ornamentation. Intricacy is an enriching technique visually, and associated with power and wealth, while economy is visually
fundamental, emphasizing the conservative and understatement of
the poor and the pure.

UNDERSTATEMENT   EXAGGERATION

Understatement (6.16) and exaggeration (6.17) are the intellectual
counterparts of economy-intricacy, serving similar ends but in a
different context. Understatement is an approach of great restraint
that seeks maximum response from the viewer from minimum ele-

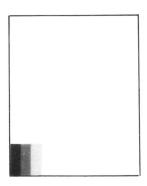

FIGURE 6.16. UNDERSTATEMENT

FIGURE 6.17. EXAGGERATION

ments. In fact, understatement in its studied attempt to engender great effect is the exact mirror image of its visual polarity, exaggeration. Both, in their own way, take great liberties with the manipulation of visual detail. Exaggeration, to be visually effective, must overstate extravagantly, enlarging its expression far beyond the truth to heighten and amplify.

PREDICTABILITY   SPONTANEITY

Predictability (6.18), as a visual technique suggests some order or plan that is highly conventional. Whether through experience or observation or reason, one should be able to foretell in advance what the entire visual message will be, based on the minimum of information. Spontaneity (6.19), on the other hand, is characterized by an apparent lack of plan. It is an emotion-fraught technique, impulsive and unconstrained.

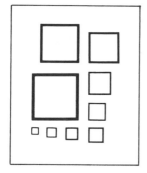  

FIGURE 6.18. PREDICTABILITY

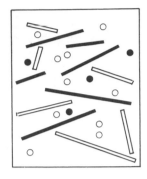

FIGURE 6.19. SPONTANEITY

ACTIVENESS   STASIS

Activity (6.20), as a visual technique, must be reflective of motion through representation or suggestion. The energetic and lively posture of an active visual technique is highly modified in the motionless

FIGURE 6.20. ACTIVENESS

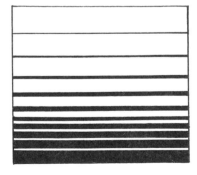

FIGURE 6.21. STASIS

force of the technique of static representation (6.21), which, through absolute equilibrium, presents an effect of quiescence and repose.

SUBTLETY   BOLDNESS
In a visual message, subtlety is the technique you would choose to make a fine distinction, shunning any obviousness and energy of purpose. While subtlety (6.22) suggests a delicate and highly refined visual approach, it must be keenly devised and ingenious in solution. Boldness (6.23) is, by its very nature, an obvious visual technique. It should be turned to by the designer with daring and used with assurance and confidence, since its purpose is to seek optimum visibility.

FIGURE 6.22. SUBTLETY

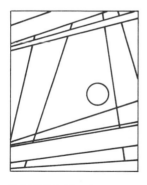

FIGURE 6.23. BOLDNESS

NEUTRALITY   ACCENT
A neutral (6.24) look to a design is almost a contradiction in terms, and yet there are occasions when the least provoking setting for a visual statement can be the most effective in cutting through viewer resistance or even belligerency. Little of the atmosphere of neutrality

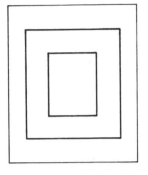

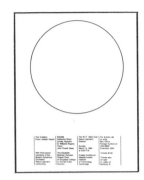

FIGURE 6.24. NEUTRALITY

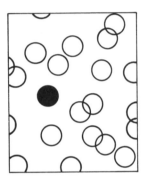

FIGURE 6.25 ACCENT

is disturbed by the technique of accent (6.25), in which just one thing is highlighted against a sameness of background.

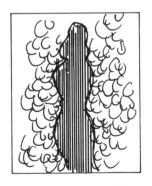
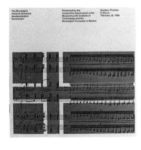
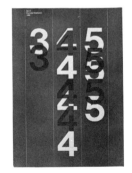

FIGURE 6.26. TRANSPARENCY

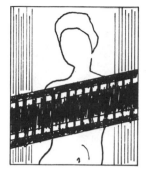

FIGURE 6.27. OPACITY

TRANSPARENCY   OPACITY

The technique polarities of transparency (6.26) and opacity (6.27) define each other physically: the former means visual detail that can be seen through so that what is behind it is revealed to the eye; the latter is just the opposite, blocking out, concealing what it visually supersedes.

CONSISTENCY   VARIATION

Consistency (6.28) is the technique for expressing visual compatibility, for developing a composition dominated by one thematic approach, uniform and consonant. If message strategy calls for changes and elaborations, the technique of variation (6.29) offers diversity and assortment. But variation, in visual composition, reflects the use of variation in musical composition in that the mutations are controlled by one dominant theme.

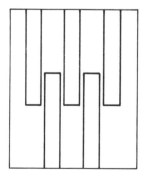

FIGURE 6.28. CONSISTENCY

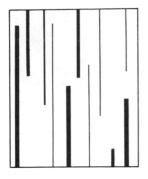

FIGURE 6.29. VARIATION

ACCURACY   DISTORTION

Accuracy (6.30) is the natural technique of the camera, the option of the artist. Our natural visual experience of things is the model of realism in the visual arts and its utilization can involve many tricks and conventions calculated to replicate the same visual cues as the eye

FIGURE 6.30. ACCURACY

FIGURE 6.31. DISTORTION

conveys to the brain. The camera is patterned on the eye and, consequently, delivers many of its effects. For the artist, the use of perspective reinforced with the technique of chiaroscuro can suggest what
we see directly in experience. But they are tricks on the eye. The
most studied accuracy in painting is called just that, a "trompe
l'oeil." Distortion (6.31) tampers with realism, seeking control of
effect through deviation from regular shape and, possibly, true form.
This is a technique that responds to strong purpose in visual composition and, well-handled, produces intense response.

FLATNESS   DEPTH
Both of these visual techniques are primarily ruled by the use or non-
use of perspective and augmented by replication of the environmental
information through imitation of the effects of light and shade
through chiaroscuro (6.32, 6.33) to suggest or to erase the natural
appearance of dimension.

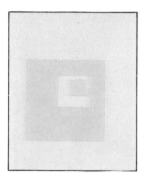  

FIGURE 6.32. FLATNESS

FIGURE 6.33. DEPTH

SINGULARITY   JUXTAPOSITION

Singularity (6.34) is the focus of a composition on one separate and solitary theme, unsupported by any other particular or general visual stimuli. The strongest quality of this technique is the specific emphasis it conveys. Juxtaposition (6.35) expresses the interaction of visual stimuli, placing, as it does, at least two cues side by side, activating comparison of relationships.

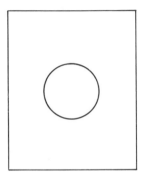
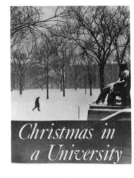

FIGURE 6.34. SINGULARITY

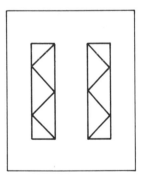

FIGURE 6.35. JUXTAPOSITION

SEQUENTIALITY   RANDOMNESS

A sequential (6.36) arrangement in design is based on the compositional response to a plan of presentation that is arranged in a logical order. The arrangement can have any formula, but usually involves a series of things set in a rhythmic pattern. A random (6.37) technique should suggest a lack of plan, or a planned disorganization or accidental presentation of visual information.

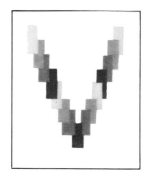

FIGURE 6.36. SEQUENTIALITY

FIGURE 6.37. RANDOMNESS

SHARPNESS   DIFFUSION

Sharpness (6.38) as a visual technique is linked closely to clarity of
physical state as well as clarity of expression. Through the use of precision and hard edges, the final effect is a distinct one and easy to in-

FIGURE 6.38. SHARPNESS

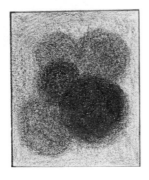

FIGURE 6.39. DIFFUSION

terpret. Diffusion (6.39) is soft, opting for less precision of character, but more atmosphere, more feeling and warmth.

REPETITION   EPISODICITY
Repetition (6.40) is the uninterrupted visual connections that are par-

FIGURE 6.40. REPETITION

FIGURE 6.41. EPISODICITY

ticularly important to any unitized visual statement. In film, in architecture, in graphics, continuity is not only the uninterrupted steps from one point to another, but it is also the cohesive force that holds a diverse composition together. Episodic techniques (6.41) in visual expression indicate the expression of disconnection or, at least, loose connections. This is a technique which reinforces the individual quality of the parts of the whole without completely abandoning the larger meaning.

These techniques are only some of the many possible information modifiers available to the designer. Almost every visual formulator has a counterforce, and each of them is connected with the control of the visual elements that result in the shaping of content, the construction of message. Many more visual techniques can be explored, discovered, and utilized compositionally, and always in the action-counteraction polar state: brightness, dullness; colorfulness, monochromaticity; angularity, roundness; verticality, horizontality; sketchiness, mechanicalness; intersection, parallelism. Their opposite states of polarity offer the visual composer great opportunity to sharpen the meaning of the work in which they are applied through the use of contrast.

Visual techniques overlap and reinforce meaning in any compositional effort; all together they present artist and nonartist alike with the most effective means of making and understanding expressive visual communication in the search for a universal visual language.

EXERCISES
1. Pick out any polar techniques (accent-neutrality, exaggeration-understatement, depth-flatness, etc.) and find as many examples of each as you can. Arrange the examples from one polarity to another.

2. Choose any one visual subject and photograph it to demonstrate as many visual techniques as you possibly can express by different camera angles and positions, as well as other technical variations including light.

3. Choose one of the techniques listed and not shown and sketch an abstract design to illustrate it.

4. Take a number of advertisements, posters, or photographs and beside each list the techniques most evident in their composition.

7
THE SYNTHESIS OF VISUAL STYLE

In the preceding chapters there is a diversity of point of view about what factors and forces the visual artist and communicator must be familiar with in order to construct, compose, pre-plan any visual material in terms of meaning or mood. Knowledge of shared principles of perception forms a stepping-off point, a base for prediction of the effect of certain visual decisions in the organization of a project. The elements offer the visual communicator the fundamental (and meaning-charged) substance for construction. Categorizing the different levels of visual input and output points the way to intelligent definition of the task and its underlying purpose. The techniques are the enablers, the options for choice that control the results. All together these visual means offer the artist another level of form and content encompassing the personal statement of the individual creator and, beyond that, the shared visual philosophy and character of a group, a culture, a period in history.

STYLE
Style is the visual synthesis of the elements, techniques, syntax, inspiration, expression, and basic purpose. It is complex and difficult to describe with clarity. Maybe the best way to establish the definition in terms of visual literacy is to regard it as a category or class of visual expression shaped by a total cultural environment. For instance, the differences between Oriental and Occidental art are the conventions that govern them. Of the two cultural styles, the Oriental is by far the more conventionalized, that is, legislated by strong rules and basic principles involving generally accepted cultural agreement. In most Japanese art, and, for that matter, life style, there is a deference to "the way." Basically this refers to the way of doing things, whether it is drawing a picture, designing a garden, preparing tea, or writing haiku. The approach to all things assumes high standards, a love of beauty, a devotion on the part of the individual who undertakes the tasks, but the concept of "the way" extends beyond these guidelines given. Its meaning can be best illustrated by describing the rules for writing haiku. The form is rigidly defined. A haiku must have seventeen syllables. No more, no less. No variations are allowed or honored. All choice of technique and individual expression must fit into the prescribed format. It is a convention. But the Japanese not only accept the absolute rules for writing this special kind of poem, they search for freedom within the imposed discipline and seem comfor-

table working within a structure. The results seem no less creative than freer poetic forms that offer subjective options. Indeed, no one could consider the haiku a potential cliché.

Style influences artistic expression in much the same way as conventions do. But stylistic rules are subtler than conventions, exerting on the creative act influence rather than control. Western artistic conventions are freer than Oriental art, yet, nevertheless, the personal style they allow for is contained within the superimposed context of cultural style. Architect Louis Sullivan felt the imposed structure this way: "You cannot express unless you have a system of expression; and you cannot have a system of expression unless you have a prior system of thinking and feeling; and you cannot have a system of thinking and feeling unless you have a basic system of living." The systems of living, for artists as well as all people, are culturally conditioned and the step-by-step definition of the broad categories of visual expression helps to understand the relationship between individual style and the precedence and dominance of cultural style.

There are many names for artistic styles that identify not only a methodology of expression, but also a period in history and a defined geographical locale: Byzantine, Renaissance, Baroque, Impressionist, Dada, Flemish, Gothic, Bauhaus, Victorian. Each name conjures up a series of recognizable visual cues that, put together, encompass the work of many artists as well as a period and a place. The similarity of the work of the Impressionists is seen as one, coherent, related, stylistic group, which in no way disturbs the recognizable individuality of each artist identified within the whole. The Victorian period may not suggest the names of a group of artists all working in the same generalized style, but there is no question that there is a richness of visual referents associated with the name. What makes this so? Each individual group, in its probing for new forms, establishes its own traditions. At the structural level, the search for new forms means experimenting with compositional orchestration of the elements, and the establishing of new traditions and results in a methodology based on choice of manipulative visual techniques. The preferences for method are shared by artists and craftsmen working within a style. It is possible, then, to pick one example from a designated style period and analyze it from the point of view of its elemental structure and the compositional decisions arrived at through the choice of enabling techniques. Refinements and variations of technique can serve to identify an individual artist's uniqueness of style, but a broad point of view in the analysis will effectively define the style of the entire school or period which encompasses his work.

Impressionism, for one, is a stylistic period associated totally with painting. It was a French school, whose members worked in and around Paris in the mid-nineteenth century. Monet's painting is an example of the elements and techniques that shape and form the entire school (7.1). The Gothic style appears not only in architectural form,

FIGURE 7.1

but also in sculpture, graphics, and crafts. It was spread across northern Europe from France to Germany to England, covering a period of time from the end of the twelfth century through the thirteenth century and, finally into the fourteenth century, a transition period characterized by highly decorated versions of the style. A pure example of Gothic style, and maybe the most famous, is the cathedral at Chartres (7.2). Again, the specific example serves as one of a class that takes so much of its form and content from the choice of techniques in its composition.

Naming a style or a school of visual expression is a great historical convenience for easy identification and reference (7.3), but in contemporary times there has been a fragmentation of nomenclature that has accelerated into a state of absurdity. From op to pop to top (ographical), the shifting of names has evolved into an almost daily occurrence, an expression unto itself. True, individuality of work is not only desirable but an inevitability for all people. Every human

FIGURE 7.2

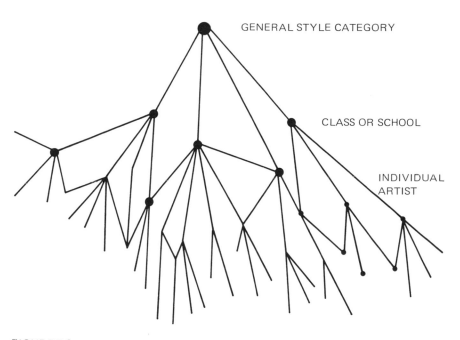

GENERAL STYLE CATEGORY

CLASS OR SCHOOL

INDIVIDUAL
ARTIST

FIGURE 7.3

has a unique face, a unique thumbprint, a unique scanning pattern,
and every human being would, if asked to draw a circle, produce a
unique circle. And yet, grouping in style does appear in the analysis
of a period in history, visually as well as philosophically. Not only

does the work of individual artists naturally group together based on the relationships of media, method, and techniques, but stylistic groups, in the same way, can relate to each other because of the similarities of form and content, even though they are widely separated in time and space, historically and geographically.

Style, in the visual arts, is the ultimate synthesis of all the forces and factors, the coming together, the annealing of many decisions and steps. At the first level is the choice of medium, and the influence of the medium on the form and content. Then, there is the purpose, the reason why something is being made: for survival, for communication, for self-expression. The actual making presents a series of options: the search for compositional decisions by means of choice of elements and recognition of elemental character; the manipulation of the elements through the choice of appropriate techniques. The final result is an individual (or sometimes group) expression monitored by many of the above factors, but mainly and most deeply, influenced by what is going on in the social and physical and political and psychological environment, all of which are crucial to everything we do or express visually.

What is the perceptual influence of outside forces on the making of all classes of visual objects and the expression of ideas? The inhabitant of a dense jungle who is accustomed to being closed in a limited space in dim light has enormous difficulty seeing in an intensely bright, flat, and open plain. The opposite formulation makes it difficult for a desert dweller, used to focusing on great distances, to see in close quarters. These are purely physiological conditions, but social patterns, the behavior of groups with and toward each other, and, as a group toward others, have enormous influence on perception and expression also. Perceptions are formed by belief, religion, and philosophy; what you believe has tremendous control over what you see. The ruling class and those who are ruled, political and economic factors, all work together to influence perception and shape expression. Altogether, politics, economics, the environment, the social patterns create a group psyche. These same kinds of forces that develop into individual languages in verbal usage, combine in the visual mode into a shared style of expression.

Almost all the products of the visual arts and crafts in man's history can be related to five broad categories of visual style: primitive, expressionistic, classical, embellished, functional. Lesser style periods

and schools relate in character to one or a few of these all-encompassing categories. To understand and accomplish these categorizations,
it is necessary to rise above stereotyped labeling to a level of arche-
typal definition. For instance, man's earliest attempts to record and
transmit information in the cave paintings of southern France and
northern Spain are frequently called primitive. As E. H. Gombrich
says in The Story of Art: "not because they are simpler than we are—
their processes of thought are often more complicated than ours—but
because they are closer to the state from which all mankind emerged."

PRIMITIVISM

Since all that remains of the primitive man's purpose when he created
drawings 30,000 years ago are the drawings themselves, we can
only conjecture about their purposes. To such men the animals in
their environment were at once a mortal threat to them and at the
same time, their means of survival. For the most part, it was these animals that were the chief subject matter of their work. Why did they
draw them, deep in the winter caves, high on the walls? Some possibilities are more favored than others. One of the qualities of the cave
paintings is their realism, an unnatural quality in primitive art, which
suggests that they were intended to be a visual aid, a hunting manual
composed to recreate the problems of the hunt and refresh the knowledge of the hunter as well as to instruct those as yet inexperienced.
This theory is supported by details of drawings with arrows pointing
to vital organs and vulnerabilities of the animals. The drawings were
amazingly lyrical of line, really quite lovely, indicating that it is likely that they were done with great love and appreciation of the animals represented. Our thirty-centuries-old cave dweller might, indeed, share some of the nostalgia for his fellow creepers as well as a
memory of warmer seasons when game was plentiful and so was the
food supply. It is possible that these works are from the hands of the
society's first Sunday painters, and it should be noted they have great
beauty and, by any standards of art, are extraordinarily sophisticated.
But the threatening environment presented to primitive man unan-
swerable questions, and not unlike most men so beset, these drawings
must have had some relationship to the mysteries he was attempting
to understand and contain and therefore must have served in some
way a quasi-religious purpose.

Certainly the animal, along with other objects from nature common
to the environment, appears prominently in primitive religions, expressing the mystical power men attached to them. Animal symbols,

called totems, differ in many ways from the cave-drawn animals. For one thing, their social purposes are more complex. Along with their religious significance, they also serve purposes of law, prohibiting incest in the simple social systems of preliterate men by making clearer family attachment of the group sharing the same totem. Clan totems took on a scientific purpose when they were used to identify the relationship of star clusters in the sky and their changing positions in the different seasons. Eventually the totems in the zodiac served as man's first calendar. These are the astrological symbols we are born under, and which some people still follow as highly significant indications of their personality and even destiny.

The only valid way to categorize these prehistoric drawings is to try to define primitive as a style, based on purpose and techniques. Primitive art and design is stylistically unsophisticated, that is, it has not developed techniques for replicating natural visual information realistically. In fact, it is a style rich in "symbols" with strongly attached meaning, and for this reason, may have a great deal more to do with the development of writing than visual expression. A sequence in the variation of the recording of visual information can be delineated, which may clarify a great deal of the ambiguous language of the visual arts. The cave painting is man's attempt to look at nature and mark it down as realistically as possible. This is drawing done by some member of the tribe with a particular ability to express what he sees graphically. It is an ability not enjoyed by all his peers. His drawing, then, becomes a language everyone can understand but not everyone can speak. The totem is usually an abstraction from nature, a simplification embodying the essence of the object. This abstract symbolization of nature can be reproduced by anyone; this is a language anyone can understand and everyone can speak. One step further is the symbol that has no connection with any object in the environment, which holds coded information and can be negotiated by anyone, like letters or numbers, but must be learned, since its meaning has been arbitrarily attached to it.

Considering that any form of literacy, that is, system of writing, is unlikely for a primitive people, it is not surprising that there is such richness of symbolism. The symbol is characteristically the shorthand of visual communciation and wherever it is used, especially in primitive art, it channels great informational energy from the creator to the audience. Other aspects of primitive art reinforce these qualities of in-

tensification of meaning. Simplicity of shape, in fact, simplicity, is a
prime visual technique of the style. Flatness of rendition is also a frequently noticable technique in primitive visual work, as are primary
colors. The sum total of all these techniques is a kind of childlike
quality in the primitive style, which has some importance to the synthesis of this style. Anton Ehrenzwieg so values this approach that he
says in The Hidden Order of Art: "nothing less than the young child's
unconcern for aesthetic detail and his headlong rush for the syncretistic whole will do." What Ehrenzweig means by "syncretistic" is a
kind of purposeful neglect of detail toward an end of grasping the
meaning in the total object. In primitive art, in the visual work of

children, as in many other art forms, syncretistic vision is a powerful and intense means of expression. A caricature is an example of the manipulation of reality of parts of a human face which altogether is more like the person depicted than a realistic portrait can show. Why? Because the unique characteristics are exaggerated and the result short-circuits the most important information available directly to the perceptions of the observer.

We judge the work of children and primitives as crude, but before we accept this judgment, we should reevaluate the work on the basis of its purpose. Appropriateness has great effect on any visual work, and the intensity and purity of this style should be given its due.

Every visual style draws its character and appearance from the visual techniques applied, whether consciously by the highly trained artist and artisan or unconsciously, as in the case of the primitive or child.

Primitive Techniques
Exaggeration
Spontaneity
Activeness
Simplicity
Distortion
Flatness
Irregularity
Roundness
Colorfulness

EXPRESSIONISM
Closely related to the primitive style is expressionism; the only major difference between the two is intention. Frequently the exaggerated detail of the primitive is part of an outreach toward representationalism, a sincere attempt to make things look more real, an attempt that fails because of the lack of techniques. Expressionism uses exaggeration purposefully to distort reality. It is a style that seeks to provoke emotion, whether religious or intellectual. Part of its roots lies in the early Christian conflict between the iconodule and the iconoclast. Early Christianity was a new religion greatly influenced by the Hebrew prohibition of image worship which was associated with false gods. The compromise was an abstraction from reality that was still recognizable. The distortion, the emphasis on emotion, makes the Byzantine a typical example of expressionistic style. Wherever it ex-

ists, the style reaches beyond the rational to the mystical, to an inner vision of reality, charged with passion and heightened by feeling.

Expressionism has always dominated the work of individual artists or whole schools, whose work can be characterized by great feeling and spirituality. The Middle Ages, for instance, produced one of the greatest examples of the style, Gothic. It was a period in history fraught with defects, typified by the Crusades, a two-hundred-year exercise in futility. But through it all, in a continuing gesture of devotion to God and a reaching for eternal salvation in heaven, the people joined their efforts to build their churches as an offering of their town and city. Supervised by master builders and craftsmen, each citizen of a town labored anonymously to make some lasting contribution to his God. The result was a slow but passionate development of the Gothic cathedral, whose pointed arches, vaulting, and flying buttresses opened up space for light to come in through stained glass windows. The attenuated upreach through the intense use of verticality of line gave anyone standing inside a sensation of being levitated, of being lifted up to heaven.

The same intensity of feeling is present in the landscapes and portraits of El Greco and Kokoschka, whose work is strongly related to the mosaics of the Byzantine Empire. Whether in the Gothic or Byzantine or the work of individual artists, expressionistic style is present when the artist or designer is seeking to evoke a maximum emotional response from the viewer.

Expressionistic Techniques
Exaggeration
Spontaneity
Activeness
Complexity
Roundness
Boldness
Variation
Distortion
Irregularity
Juxtaposition
Verticality

CLASSICISM
The emotionalism of expressionism is a direct contrast to the rationality of design methodology typical of Greek and Roman art, which produced the prototypic visual style of classicism. In its purest form, classical style derives its inspiration from two sources. First, it is influenced by a love of nature, which was idealized by the Greeks to a kind of super reality. Instead of seeing themselves, as the Judeo-Christians did, as the emissaries of God on earth, they worshipped many gods with varying and specialized powers as supermen, often in pursuit of extremely worldly pleasures. The Greeks searched for pure truth in their philosophy and science, and here lay the second sources for the classical style. They formalized their art through mathematics,

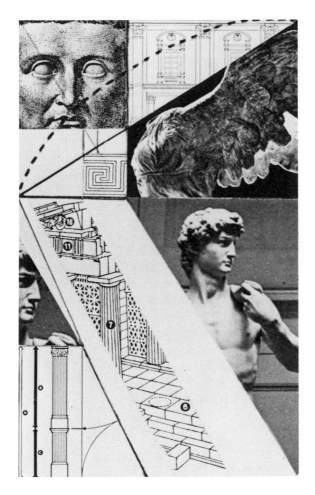

developing a formula for guiding design decisions called the Golden
Mean. The visual elegance they sought was tied to this system, but
the rigidity it produced was heightened by their perfection of execu-
tion and softened by the warming effects of the decorative sculpture,
the painting and the artifacts that enhanced their formula understructure. The Greeks sought beauty in reality. They glorified man and his
natural environment. They cherished thought. Their efforts have produced a visual style with rationality and logic in art and design.

Greece and Rome were the source of the "Renaissance," a period
whose name meant just that, a rebirth of the classical tradition. The

fifteenth-century Italian scholars and artists studied every treasured remnant of those cultures, and under their influence, turned their attention away from the Christian themes of the Middle Ages to humanism. Although the artists and craftsmen were focused on the Greco-Roman version of classical style, the Renaissance was, in fact, an individual expression of the same theme. Like their predecessors, they admired reality, and through the development of perspective and a unique way to treat light in painting, they succeeded in their painting in replicating the environment as though it were reflected in a mirror. It is no coincidence that the first glimmerings of the future invention of photography originated in the Renaissance in the form of the camera obscura, a plaything used to reproduce the environment on a wall in a darkened room.

In both the fifteenth and the sixteenth centuries, the visual artist left his anonymous role to be recognized, not only as an individual, but as a master, whose education had to be that of a classical scholar. Perfection was, then, as it will always be, associated with the classical style. Like the Greco-Roman culture, the Renaissance was a great watershed of ideas, artistic and philosophical, a period of great genius.

Classical Techniques
Harmony
Simplicity
Accuracy
Symmetry
Sharpness
Monochromaticity
Depth
Consistency
Stasis
Unity

THE EMBELLISHED STYLE
The embellished style is one that emphasizes the softening of hard edges with discursive visual techniques to produce a warming and elegant effect. Not only is the style itself rich in its complexities of design, but it is associated with wealth and power. The grandiose effects it can produce are an abandonment of reality for theatrical decoration, the world of fantasy. In other words, the nature of the style is often florid and overstated, the perfect setting for emperor or king living without concern for much beyond his own indulgences. There

are many periods and schools of art and design that can be grouped
under the overall identification of embellishment: Art Nouveau, Victorian, Late Roman. In each case, the designs are typically grandiose,
with endless surface decoration, seemingly ruled by the dictum: the
most desirable connection between two dots is a curved line.

No school is more representative of the qualities of this style than the
Baroque. This period served as a bridge between the Renaissance and
the modern era, spreading its style from its Italian origins north of
the Alps to Flanders, Germany, to England, to France, to central
Europe, to Spain and, carried by Catholic missionaries, to Latin
America and the Far East. While the Renaissance was both Italian and,

for the most part, homogeneous. Baroque art is a very inadequate, generalized category under which to group so vast and varied a period of
creative expression covering the seventeenth and eighteenth centuries.
But inadequate though it may be, it does describe a time of anachro-
nism, of great wealth juxtaposed with great poverty. There certainly
seemed to be no premium on objectivity or even reality at any level.

The lushness of Baroque certainly seems to bear little relationship to
the Victorian period, and yet they both share the same stylistic category. Clearly their inspiration for embellishment differs. For one culture, unrestrained decoration was the symbolic posture of power and
glory, while for the Victorian period, it was more of an orgy of home-
ly curliques.

Embellished Techniques
Complexity
Intricacy
Exaggeration
Roundness
Boldness
Fragmentation
Variation
Colorfulness
Activeness
Brightness

FUNCTIONALITY

While functionality has been associated primarily with contemporary
design, it is, in fact, as old as the first pot that was ever made to hold
water. It is a design methodology most closely connected to the rule
of utility and economic consideration. The advent of the Industrial
Revolution and technological development has linked the philosophy
of simple means to the natural capability of the machine, even though
the simple means has always been available to making and manufacture. The major change from other visual stylistic approaches and the
functional style is the seeking of beauty in the thematic and expressive qualities of the basic and underlying structure in any visual work.

Finding aesthetic value in workmanship is not new. It is typical of
any craftsman who delights in the imperfections that have to do with
the struggle between him and his medium. The very people who first
developed a modern philosophy of craftsmanship, the Pre-Raphael-

ites, did it on the basis of rejecting the whole concept of manufacture by machine. In England, led by William Morris, the Arts and Crafts Council espoused a philosophy that held "Truth in making is making by hand, and making by hand is making by joy." They chose to turn their backs on the distasteful reality of mass production. But whether or not they liked it was unimportant—the machine was here to stay. The first group that really tried to understand the implications of the machine and tried to cope with its potential was a loose confederation of architects, designers, and craftsmen, who lived and worked in Germany before World War I. They called themselves the "Deutscher Werkbund," and they attempted to become more aware of the inner meaning and quality of what they designed by seeking the "Sachlich-

keit" or thingness of their materials. Their probing for a means to
reconcile the artist and the machine became the inspiration for the
"Bauhaus," an art school started by Walter Gropius and a distinguished
group of teachers in Germany directly after the ending of the war, in
1919. Its purpose was to pursue new forms and new solutions to
man's basic needs as well as his aesthetic ones. The Bauhaus' curriculum returned to fundamentals, the basic materials, the basic rules of
design. And the questions they dared to ask led to new definitions of
beauty in the unadorned and practical aspects of the functional.

Functional Techniques
Simplicity
Symmetry
Angularity
Predictability
Consistency
Sequentiality
Unity
Repetition
Economy
Subtlety
Flatness
Regularity
Sharpness
Monochromaticity
Mechanicalness

There is much more to the structure and meaning of style than can
be covered solely in terms of categories or the techniques that figure
largely in developing those categories. For purposes of aesthetic definition or practical application, simplification of both style concepts
and variations of techniques is helpful in understanding and controlling the visual means. But simplification does not affect the complexity of visual literacy. The categorization exercise is purely arbitrary
and the numbers of techniques are endless in their subtle variations.
As they are treated here, they are only a hint of the vast resources of
our visual vocabulary. But the inexperienced, the visually illiterate,
must have a point of departure that will work, and knowledge of the
character of all the components of visual communication offers a
means for seeking design methods that offer some assurance of sound
solution.

EXERCISES

1. Do an abstract drawing or collage that expresses a basic style category and combines the visual techniques most prominent in it. You can use collage techniques, but avoid representational visual information.

2. Using the above exercise as inspiration shoot some photographs or find reproductions of photographs which express the style being analyzed.

3. Make a list of specific examples that identify the five different visual styles in any of the following areas: architecture, clothes design, interior design. If possible, find examples that illustrate your assumptions. Can you do the same with classes of life in nature such as trees or birds?

4. Make a sketch plan for how you might photograph the same subject in a variety of styles. Review the techniques you would use.

8
THE VISUAL ARTS:
FUNCTION AND MESSAGE

What are the basic and underlying reasons for the creation (designing, making, constructing, manufacturing) of all the many forms of visual materials? The circumstances are many, sometimes clear and direct, sometimes multilateral and overlapping. The prime motivating factor is the response to need, but the range of human needs covers an enormous area. They may be immediate and practical, having to do with the mundane matters of daily living, or they may be concerned with loftier needs for self-expression of a mood or an idea. Love of beauty, for instance, can inspire the decoration of an object in a modest and personal way or a grandiose plan for a whole environment carefully conceived for a total aesthetic effect. Many objects in the visual mode are meant to glorify or memorialize an individual or group, sometimes monumental in scope, more often modest. But so much of the visual material produced has only to do with a response to the need to record, preserve, or replicate and identify people, places, objects, or classes of visual data. Such materials are enormously useful for demonstrating and teaching both formally and informally. The last motivating reason and broadest in scope is the utilization of all levels of the visual data to extend the process of human communication.

Visual data can convey information: specific messages or expressive feelings, either by intention and for a defined purpose or obliquely and and as a by-product of utility. One thing is certain, in all the world of visual media, even including the most casual and offhand forms—some kind of information is present, whether artfully fashioned or casually produced. At whatever level in the constantly shifting evaluation of what is fine or applied art, every conceivable visual form has an incomparable ability to inform the observer either about himself and his own world, or about other times and other places, faraway and unfamiliar. This is the most unique and invaluable characteristic of a wide range of seemingly unrelated visual formats.

A visual medium can fulfill multiple roles at once. For instance, a poster designed primarily to announce a piano performance may ultimately serve as decoration on a wall of a study, its primary communication purpose superseded. An abstract painting, totally subjectively conceived by an artist, an expression of the artist's feelings, may be

effectively used as a background cover design of a fund-raising booklet produced by a charitable organization. The purposes of visual media mesh, interact, and change with kaleidoscopic complexity. To understand the visual media, our knowledge of them must be based on
a broad point of view. The answers to why they are planned and produced are fluid, and therefore the questions must be too. They must
probe the character of each medium, its function or levels of function,
its appropriateness, its natural constituency, and lastly, its history
and how it serves societal needs.

SOME UNIVERSAL ASPECTS OF VISUAL COMMUNICATION

There are many reasons for considering the potential of visual literacy. Some are triggered by the limitations of verbal literacy. Reading
and writing and their relationship to education are still a luxury of
the richer and more technologically developed nations of the world.
For the illiterate, there remains spoken language, the picture and the
symbol as the main communication means, and of these, only the visual can be preserved in any practical fashion. In this circumstance,
the visual communicator has distinct importance. This is as true today as it has ever been in history. In the Middle Ages and the Renaissance, the artist served the Church as a vital propagandist. In stained
glass windows, statuary, carvings, frescoes, paintings, illustrations of
manuscripts, he delivered "the Word" in visual form to an audience
which, through their efforts, saw the Biblical stories in palpable form.
Indeed, the visual communicator has served emperor and commissar.
The "social realism" style of the Russian revolution demonstrated
some of the facts of visual communication to an illiterate and probably unsophisticated public. In films such as Ten Days that Shook the
World or Potemkin, Eisenstein used actual newsreel inserts, but in his
original material he followed documentary techniques for a quality
of authenticity, designed to persuade and convince the audience that
it was an eyewitness to history. In illustration and painting and design, the Russians follow the same technique of superrealism toward
the same end. Both cases respond to the fact that pictorial communication directed at low literacy groups must be simple and realistic to
be effective. Subtlety and sophistication tend to be counterproductive. A fine balance must be sought: neither oversimplification, that
is, deletion of important details, nor complexity, the introduction of
unnecessary details, will extend and reinforce comprehension. Simplified realism was the same approach used by a dazzling array of Mexi-
can artists, Siqueros, Orozco, Rivera, to carry their government's mes-

sage of social revolution. They, and many other artists, revived fresco painting and used it to decorate the walls of provincial villages with paintings whose prime purpose was political propaganda. Visual means for education have been utilized in the population control campaign in India; in identification of political parties all over the world; in political indoctrination in Cuba. Among illiterate constituencies, visual communication's effectiveness is undisputed.

But the implications of the universal quality of visual information does not stop at the point of using it as a stand-in for verbal information. The two are not in conflict. Each has unique capabilities, and yet it is the visual mode that has not been wholly utilized. Visual understanding is a natural means that does not have to be learned, but rather, through visual literacy, only refined. What we see is not, as it is in language, a surrogate that has to be translated from one state to another. In perceptual terms, what is an apple for an American is an apple for a Frenchman, even though the latter calls it "une pomme." But like language, effective visual communication should avoid ambiguity of visual cues and attempt to express ideas in the simplest, most direct way. It is through oversophistication and the choice of complex symbolism that cross-cultural difficulties can arise in visual communication.

There have been many attempts to develop systems that would reinforce universal visual literacy. One is a visual counterpart of a dictionary which uses extremely simple and diagrammatic pictures instead of words as an attempt to establish conformity of visual data. This pictogram system is called ISOTYPE, a contraction of its full name, International System of Typographic Picture Education. The collection consists of a vast series of cartoonlike drawings of familiar objects which are designed to be recognized at a glance by emphasizing the most important features of what they depict. As yet, this system, or others like it, has not been widely used. Its significance for use on visual computers as an advanced form of international sign language has yet to emerge.

The Paris cartoonist, Jean Effel, has attempted to develop another kind of system for universal visual communication, a kind of visual "esperanto," which he designed to take advantage of the multiple symbol systems already in world currency. An example of what he is trying to achieve demonstrates the possibilities of such a system. See if you can read it visually.

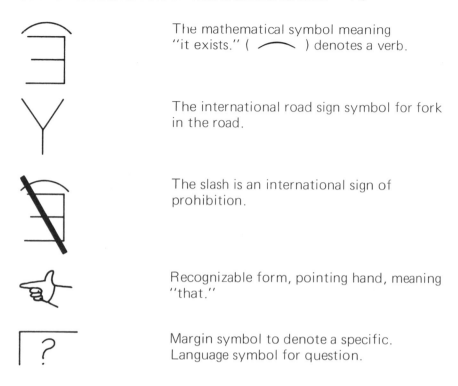

The mathematical symbol meaning "it exists." (⌒) denotes a verb.

The international road sign symbol for fork in the road.

The slash is an international sign of prohibition.

Recognizable form, pointing hand, meaning "that."

Margin symbol to denote a specific. Language symbol for question.

The message is from Shakespeare's <u>Hamlet</u>, "To be or not to be, that is the question."

The major problem in Effel's system, as opposed to ISOTYPE, is that it is just a newer version of any language based on pictograph or abstract symbols. All its visual clues are surrogates and must be translated to have meaning. In other words, Effel is really inventing another language which ignores that special quality of visual information, spontaneous evidence. It is this quality, the direct apprehension of visual information, that adds one more dimension to the desirability of visual data as communication media: the extraordinary ability to express many pieces of information all at once, instantly.

Through visual expression, we are able to frame a direct statement; through visual perception, we experience a direct interpretation of what we are seeing. All the individual units of visual stimuli interact, creating a mosaic of forces charged with meaning, but a special kind of meaning, unique to visual literacy, one that can be absorbed directly with comparative effortlessness compared to the slow decoding of language. Visual intelligence conveys information with amazing speed, and, if the data is clearly organized and stated, it is not only easier to absorb, it is also easier to retain and utilize referentially.

The most direct, if informal, of all visual media, is one that we all participate in, consciously or not, facial expression and body gesture. A sour taste will evoke the same reaction the world over, a distortion of the muscles of the face. Add fear to the same expression and it communicates the distress of pain. The sneer, the smile, the nod, all are variations of expression, universal in meaning, that can transcend national borders, different cultures, strange languages. The Italians have a vast language of curses, all expressed with colorful facial expressions and gestures. So do other ethnic groups. Although it was an American invention, almost anywhere in the world a driver recognizes the fist with thumb extended as a plea for a ride. The fist, thumb closed, arm aloft, is a symbol of communist unity; hand extended, palm down, arm at an angle, is the fascist salute borrowed from the ancient Roman legions by the Italian Fascisti and later appropriated by Hitler's brownshirted Nazis. All these are related to a simple and basic language of communication used by men, even animals (surely we all know what a dog means when he wags his tail), to communicate visually. Manipulation of the hands forms the alphabet of the deaf, but most expressions and gestures are far less formalized and exist only as a kind of folk language. Gesture and expression in the dance and theater are called by other names—dancing, acting—and in this context, they are considered art.

Gesture, expression, written language, symbolization are all within the scope of the layman. But the visual arts, crafts, industrial design, photography, painting, sculpture, architecture require practitioners with unique talent and special training. Each visual medium has not only its own special structural elements but also a unique methodology for the application of compositional decisions and utilization of techniques in their conceptualization and formulation. Understanding these forces increases the areas of experimentation and interpretation for both originator and viewer toward a more visually literate set of criteria of judgment, which can bring the making and meaning more closely together.

SCULPTURE
The essence of sculpture is that it is constructed of solid materials and exists in three dimensions. Most other visual art forms—painting,

drawing, graphics, photography, film—only suggest three dimensions by highly refined use of perspective and the light and shade of chiaroscuro. Our fingertips placed on a painting or photograph would supply no information about the physical formation of its subject matter, yet the evolution of the two-dimensional representation of three-dimensional objects has conditioned us to accept the illusion of form that has, in truth, only been suggested. But in sculpture the form is there; it can be touched, read, or understood by the sightless. Lorenzo Ghiberti, the Florentine sculptor and painter, observed, "the perfection of such works escapes the eye and can only be understood if we pass over the planes and curves of the marble with our hands." While the "do not touch" signs make the tactile experience of sculpture nearly impossible, the dimensional quality can be experienced just by seeing.

Like the rest of our world in nature, sculpture exists in a form which, in addition to being touched, can also be viewed from infinitely many angles, each plane corresponding to what, in two dimensions, would be be a complete drawing. This enormous complexity must be melded together into a structure so unified that, as Michelangelo observed, it should be possible to roll a piece of sculpture down a hill without breaking off any segment of the whole. Although stone or marble, from which sculpture is carved, is strong material, it is also brittle. Delicateness of detail is not possible; cohesiveness in the design is mandatory. Michelangelo's awareness of this fact disciplined his conception of a work. He thought of the piece as already existing within the stone, and saw the problem of the sculptor as releasing it into reality. Nowhere in the art of sculpture is this philosophy better demonstrated than in his figures, so aptly named the "Slaves," designed for the tomb of Pope Julius (8.1). In each figure of this series, Michelangelo demonstrates the process of sculpture; the rough-cut blocking out of the general shapes, the searching for more descriptive information in the form, and finally the highly detailed and polished marble softened into almost living, breathing tissue in the finished state. This effect is heightened by contrast, for each of these figures is in various and multiple states of completion, a finished and detailed hand flowing out of a rough-hewn, blocked-out arm emerging from the untouched marble, the juxtaposition intensifying each state. The figures not only emerge from the stone through Michelangelo's searching skill, but also, almost with a will of their own, seem to be straining against the marble for release. Of the six figures originally planned for the tomb, only two were finished. The other four are in the Academia in

FIGURE 8.1

Florence, and, in this unique state of being finished, partly finished and untouched, they represent a complete and incomparable study of how sculpture is conceived and accomplished.

The word sculpture comes from sculpere, to carve, although the second most favored method of sculpture is not carving but a building up process, using soft materials such as clay or wax. This allows greater chance for experimentation and change, the work being completely unfixed in the process of construction, so that mistakes can be corrected without difficulty. When the work is finished, the soft clay can be translated to the final state in two ways. It can be fired (baked at very high temperature) and hardened into a material called terracotta, or it can be cast in molds into plastic or a permanent metal, the most common being bronze. This method makes possible delicacy and fluidity of expression unattainable in brittle stone.

Except for bas-relief, which is a braille-like bridge between the two-dimensional and the true three-dimensional form, sculpture must be controlled through compactness of design. Whether emphasizing the glorified human figure in the noblest hour of Greece's classical period, or accenting the spirituality of man in the expressionistic figures which were an integral part of the architecture of the Middle Ages, simplicity is the most necessary ingredient of the effectiveness of sculpture.

Planning a three-dimensional work entails two-dimensional sketches that must probe around the edges and attempt to think from every angle (8.2). For a sculpture that will be carved, either in stone or wood, the design must be concentrated on the broad blocking of masses rather than detail and refinement. These additional considerations are suggested and evolved at a later stage of development. The key concern must be sensing the material from a general form to the more specific visual information.

FIGURE 8.2

The same observation may be made of the clay or wax sculpture with the emphatic noting that a far freer process of exploration and trying out of solutions is possible. The clay or wax can be put on or taken off so that, although line sketches may be used, the process of putting on and taking off is itself a sketch that moves from rough and loose interpretation toward a more and more finished stage (8.3). Some

sculptors who work in clay take this progression toward a highly finished and realistic finished state, while others, Jacob Epstein for instance, have a greater preference for leaving the textural richness of
the process as a part of the quality of the work.

A clay model can be used in the carving of large stone or marble
work through the use of calipers or other measuring devices. Sometimes the artist does the carving while sometimes specialists in
reproduction carve the finished piece from an original. This is especially true in the production of very large monuments in which scale is
the most important element of interpretation. But a piece of sculpture which looses the interpretive hand of the artist or designer in
the production process loses a quality of integrity as well.

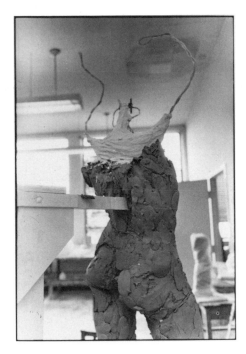

FIGURE 8.3

Modern methods of producing sculpture extend from the realistic information drawn from the environment to less and less natural information on to absolute abstraction with emphasis on pure form dominated by the visual elements of shape and dimension.

Abstraction, semi-abstraction, mobility in the basic design, new materials, and old materials used new ways, are the characteristic developments of contemporary sculpture. Even in the most experimental efforts, modern works retain the essential character of the art form, dimension that can be seen and touched. Sculpture must exist in space.

ARCHITECTURE

Architecture shares with sculpture the quality of dimension. In architecture, the dimension encloses a space whose primary purpose is to protect man from the vagaries of his environment. A building of any sort is a composition problem in pure visual elements of tone, shape, texture, scale, and dimension. The basic social unit, a sheltered place where man can sleep, prepare food, eat, work, stay warm and safe, is the house. Variations on the house—group housing and apartments— were first developed by the Romans to suit densely populated urban conditions and have their origins in caves and cliffside dwellings of tribal groups.

As cultures become more developed, the art and technique of building also serve man's activities and interests: his religion with churches, shrines, monuments, tombs; his government with administration buildings, legislatures, court houses; his leisure with theaters, auditoriums, sports arenas, museums; his welfare and education with hospitals, schools and universities, libraries.

The style and form of public and private buildings communicate beyond their social functions expressing the taste and aspirations of the social groups and institutions that designed and built them. Styles in architecture vary not only with the purpose of a building but also with the traditions of a culture, traditions often influenced by national, geographic, religious, and intellectual differences. The patterns that derive from these influences are in a constant state of flux that generates modified variations in design and, sometimes, complete innovation. Availability of material influences the character of a culture's architectural style as does knowledge of building techniques. Together, the methods and materials of building express through the construction of homes, multiple dwellings, and public buildings, the spirit and posture of a people and time and therefore hold enormous meaning. Many of the forms develop symbolic meaning: the spire, reaching for heaven; the dome, representing the sky and the heavens;

the tower, signifying power; shutters and bay windows, suggesting a cozy and protected retreat.

The architect's own preference and taste override the technics, materials, and symbolic styles. He is the artist, the conceptualizer, who draws on the basic elements of design, the current and historical styles, the materials and engineering. His architectural decisions are modified by his strongest discipline, the ultimate purpose of the building, the appropriateness of his designs. Primarily then, his buildings must stand erect to fulfill their purpose, be permanent. These demands on the craftsmanship and artistry of the architect, along with the demands of his client, limit his own subjective expression. The more utilitarian the purposes of a building, the more intense the limitations. Despite the limitations, despite the overwhelming problems of urban explosion and renewal building, the architect continues to produce meaningful, environmental designs, constantly reinterpreting

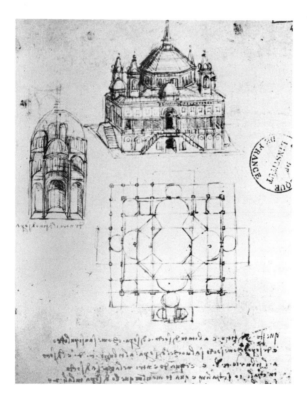

FIGURE 8.4

man's practical needs as well as expressing his culture through expression and content in architecture.

The primary planning element of architectural expression is line. Both in preliminary exploration in search of solution and in the final stages of production the linear quality of visual preparation dominates the proceedings. The first sketches may be free and undisciplined in the rough plan, searching for spatial forms in the previsualization process (8.4).

The more rigorous steps in architectural planning require detailed and structurally knowledgeable floor plans and elevations (8.5). The floor plans assign actual interior space, placement of windows, doors and other structural detail. In addition the plan must be in accurate scale and proportion so that the builder and owner can follow them and be able to project what the final results will be (8.6). Because there has to be some training in visualizing the plan in three dimensions and not all people can project the effect from blueprints or two-dimensional elevations, architects often prepare and present a client with three-dimensional renderings and, in some cases, actual three-dimensional models so that the need for visualization of something that does not yet exist except in a plan is minimized.

An architect must be an artisan and engineer who knows the methods of building and the manipulation of materials. He must be a politician, able to deal with clients from individuals to industry and government. He must be a sociologist, capable of understanding his own culture and creating designs that respond to the needs of his times and

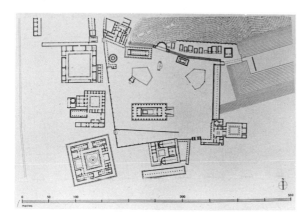

FIGURE 8.5

FIGURE 8.6

conform cohesively to the environment. Most difficult of all, he must be an artist, knowing the elements and techniques and styles of the visual arts and able to mesh form and function toward intended effects. In this area, his talents must challenge those of the sculptor, since ultimately his designs will stand as abstract visual statements to be judged aesthetically.

PAINTING

When we use the words "fine art" today, we are usually referring to painting, portable pictures hung on walls in private homes, public buildings, or museums. This ultimate visual art form has derived from many sources, starting with the earliest attempts of man in prehistory to make pictures, drawn or painted, to the contemporary art scene with its "establishment" of critic and museum and its standards for recognition and success. Primitive drawings with earth colors have survived in the caves of southern France and northern Spain as examples of the earliest attempts of man to use pictures as a means for recording and imparting information. From the beginning of civilization, picture making has been an integral part of man's life, and from it, man has developed written language. Sketches, religious objects, decorated furniture, mosaics, painted pottery and tiles, stained glass windows, tapestries, all are related to painting, and parallel writing in their ability to tell stories. But picture making, in all its forms, shares other attributes; the contemplation of nature, a way for man to see and understand himself, the glorification of groups or individuals, the expression of religious feeling, and decoration to make man's environment more pleasing.

The artist and his gift for making pictures has traditionally inspired awe, but the use of that gift in association with religious ritual adds

an aura of magic that has never completely faded from his image.
Each culture has interpreted differently the role of the artist in religious expression. Some, the Moslem and Hebrew, for example, have
prohibited it, labeling image making as antireligious, and associating
it with the worship of false gods. These instances are certainly the exception. Almost every religion, major or minor, turned to the artist to
create objects of worship, gods in the form of men, animals, the
moon, the sun, insects, flowers, even abstract symbolic configura-
tions. The style of drawing and painting tended toward the nonrealis-
tic, the exaggerated and mysterious, but the emerging classical tradition of the Greeks changed this with its emphasis on man, primarily,
and constituting gods as kind of supermen. This demanded realism in
artistic expression, the understanding of the demands of perspective,
and knowledge of anatomy that required careful study of nature. Inevitably, the plastic arts shifted away from the early Christian style
of distortion and expressionism toward the essence of Greek spirit,
the direct and rational. The classic style was inherited by Rome, and
along with it, the emphasis on realism, mathematical proportion, and
monument, leaving little for the painter but the murals on the walls
of public buildings and the villas of the rich, and some portraiture as
the limited area in which he could practice his craft.

The collapse of the Roman empire echoed in the rise of the Christian
world. Still grappling with the Hebrew tradition which prohibited
"graven images," the early Christians rejected realism and returned to
expressionism in drawing and painting for a highly charged emotional effect. The mosaics of the Byzantine churches and the stained glass
windows of the Gothic cathedrals intertwined with the flat, nondi-
mensional style of painting, rich in mysticism, until the Renaissance
rediscovered the classical tradition. Here, the two styles fused in a
search for both the emotional and rational response. A burst of interest in anatomy and perspective combined with an increase of patron-
age, and painting became a major art form from then on, to be considered one of the most important expressions of man's spirit. Painting
came down from the walls of buildings, and shifted from its role as
an integral part of architecture, and became an entity unto itself.
Finding its origins in movable altars and religious decorations, the easel painting took the form we know today. The artist achieved a new
position in the social structure, sought after, celebrated, rich with
commisions, while his work reached out to a constantly widening audience, fulfilling all the purposes of picture making, storytelling, ob-
jectifying man and his experience, glorifying the Church and cele-

brated, and enhancing the environment. A golden age of painting of many styles ensued.

Having reached this plateau of accomplishment, the painter increasingly disassociated himself from participation and involvement in the social and economic fabric of his times. In different countries for different reasons, conditions contributed to the dichotomy between painter and society. Identifying with the Reformation and the political upheaval of the Age of Enlightenment, the artist frequently became spokesman for unpopular causes, losing his support from the "establishment." On the heels of political revolution came the Industrial Revolution and the rising standard of living of the middle class, which was countered in direct ratio by a low standard of taste, compounded by the questionable quality of mass-produced artifacts.

The Industrial Revolution brought one dynamic change to all things made by machine, craftsman, and artist; no longer were they produced on commission, but rather on speculation. Here is the product, created or manufactured; will someone want it? All of the give-and-take between maker and user, then, is broken down, giving way to a more tenuous means of understanding. All sorts of artificial approaches to inspiring consumer demand, such as advertising and market research, fill the gap, but the final test must be consumer response.

The camera took away from the artist the uniqueness of his talent. Even those who sought the painter and his products watered down their demands and daring, allowing the artist to move into an "ivory tower," sharing with him the notion, now generally accepted, that "fine art" should fulfill no other purpose than the artist's own desire for creation. Nikolaus Pevsner describes this erosive evolution in his book, Pioneers of Modern Design:

"Schiller was the first to form a philosophy of art which made him the high priest in a secularized society. Schelling took this up and Coleridge, Shelley and Keats followed, the artist is no longer a craftsman, no longer a servant, he is now a priest. Humanity may be his gospel, or beauty, a beauty 'identical with truth' (Keats), a beauty that is 'the completest unity of life and form' (Schiller). In creating the artist makes conscious 'the essential, the universal, the aspect and expression of the indwelling spirit of Nature' (Schelling). Schiller assures him: 'The dignity of Mankind is laid into thy hands,' and compares him to a king 'living on the summits of Mankind.' The inevitable consequence of such adulation became more and more visible

as the nineteenth century unfolded. The artist began to despise utility and the public. He shut himself from the real life of his time, with-
drawing into his sacred circle and creating art for art's sake, art for
the artist's sake.''

Art, any art, is the manifestation of man's yearning toward spiritual
fulfillment. To be valid, art must never cease to communicate to and
for these aspirations. As a distillation of life, it must refine truth to
the irreducible minimum, and then project it, with powerful statement, rich in universal meaning, to all levels of society. When an art
is overesoteric, and no longer maintains its ability to communicate,
its purposes, even its validity must be questioned. Possibly, those that
expound most knowledgeably, the experts, may be admiring the ''Emperor's clothes,'' fearful of appearing foolish by confronting the obvious nakedness of purpose in contemporary painting. Discernment,
taste, judgment can go by the board in the excitement of discovery,
but when science, through experiment, breaks through old concepts,
newly discovered data is connected with man's hope for progress. In
painting, it merely creates a new and more select in-group and art becomes more and more marginal to our lives, an art described by An-
dré Gide as suiting ''an impatient public and speculative dealers.''

How can society and the artist be reconciled? In the nineteenth century, William Morris envisioned a cure through denying the machine.
We will save the future, he declaimed, by marching backward into
the past, where art and man served each other. The Bauhaus philosophy dealt more realistically with the here-to-stay existence of the
machine, advocating that it be met on its own terms by art through
an emphasis on utility and economy of means. Neither approach, nor
any other, has bridged the widening gap between the artist and his
commitment to his own time. Painting continues to be more and
more esoteric. The public reacts less and less to each artist's attempt
to express his own thoughts to himself in experiment for experiment's
sake. The painter and a society that desperately needs his special insights and peculiar talents are unreconciled in museum or suburb, and
painting and the painter drift further away from meaning and content.
''It should be clear, then'' says Edgar Wind in Art and Anarchy, ''that
by moving into the margin, art does not lose its quality as art, it only
loses its direct relevance to our existence: it becomes a splendid super-
fluity.''

But the artist, the painter, the maker of pictures has qualities of control of the media that make that product still a desirable and neces-

sary part of human experience. While the prephotography product from the painters brush supplies us with visual reports on how things looked and what people wore and all the visual information we have come to depend on the camera for, painters did more than that. They gave us insight, in measure with their ability and perceptiveness. The method for developing a drawing or painting demonstrates seeking control of the medium. First a series of sketches, from life or imagination, are developed to investigate the visual material to be included in the painting (8.7). Then a compositional structure is developed

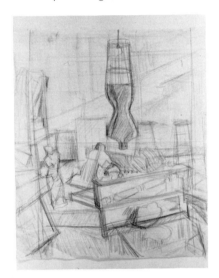

FIGURE 8.7

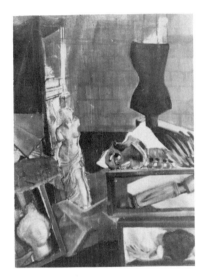

FIGURE 8.8

adapting the visual material to the abstract elemental intention of the artist (8.8). Almost all of the visual elements are represented in a painting—line, shape, tone, color, texture, scale and, by suggestion and implication, dimension and movement. The composition incorporates the process of manipulation of the elements through the use of techniques toward a planned effect. Control of all this is in the ability of the painter to plan and previsualize as well as render and produce. The artist can put in what is not there and take out what is, a capability not afforded the photographer in quite as free a way. Unlike the camera's indiscriminate though dazzling reportorial accuracy, the maker of pictures can modify the actual circumstances even to the point of abstraction of detailed information to the purer visual terminology of formal meaning.

ILLUSTRATION   163

How much influence there is in the process and product of contemporary painting is a debatable question and one that may not be resolved in the moment. One thing is certain: the human animal is a maker of pictures and however that fact is manifest, in whatever medium, for whatever purpose, it will continue to be true.

ILLUSTRATION

The massive production of books and periodicals brought about by increased technical perfection of reproduction in printing created a new field for artists to participate in—illustration. As an illustrator, the trained easel painter often served as the visualizer for the printing industry, as yet unable to reproduce and print photographs. While such superb photographers as Brady and Sullivan doggedly worked at documenting the Civil War, it was the work of illustrators that reported the war. Their sketches, made on the battlefields, were hastily engraved in metal or cut into wood to be used in the magazines and newspapers.

When techniques for reproducing photographs were developed, newspapers used them exclusively, completely abandoning the artist-illustrator. Only books (technical books and the burgeoning field of children's books), magazines, and advertising still lean heavily on the illustrator and his special ability to control his subject matter. The essentially light touch of the illustrator, the artistry of his work, is his greatest appeal. In books or magazines, fiction and fantasy are the special province of his imagination.

While easel painters do illustrating (Winslow Homer was among that band of artists who covered the Civil War), illustrators, like graphic designers, are specialists devoted to their own field. Often an illustrator is so successful and well known that a whole period is identified with him: Beardsley and the Art Nouveau of the fin de siècle; John Held, Jr., and the flapper of the American twenties; Norman Rockwell and a generation of Saturday Evening Post covers. The illustrator must achieve the same standards of excellence in draftsmanship and painting technique as the painter; in fact, he must have even more facility and speed. He must work on assignment; he must be able to create his assignment and do it for the publishing deadlines. The demands on him are trying, but the rewards are high. For all of his abilities, the illustrator is characteristically unpretentious and sometimes, as in the case of Norman Rockwell, totally disinterested in being called an artist.

There is another breed of illustrator, who has figured rather importantly in the technological advances of our time, usually of a scientific nature. It is this technological illustrator that William Ivins comments on in his book, Prints and Visual Communication:

"In the nineteenth century informative books usefully illustrated with accurately repeatable pictorial statements became available to the mass of mankind in western Europe and America. The result was the greatest revolution in practical thought and accomplishment that has ever been known. This revolution was a matter as momentous from the ethical and political points of view as from the mechanical and economic ones. The masses had begun to get the one great tool they most needed to enable them to solve their own problems."

This encyclopedic compilation of visual information started with the development of written language, and is continually expanding.

The camera, and its immeasurable ability to report visual detail, has continually made inroads on the domain of the illustrator. In any instance when believability is a factor, the photograph is preferred, even though it is quite easy to exaggerate with the camera. But television and the taste and responses of the public have all figured in the diminishing domain of the illustrator.

But whether with a photograph, a detailed line drawing, or a black-and-white or full-color halftone rendering, the illustrators main purpose is referential. It is primarily a job of bringing planned visual information to an audience, visual information usually meant to expand on a verbal message. So the variety of illustrations ranges from detailed drawings of machinery developed to explain their workings all the way to expressive drawings done by talented and accomplished artists to accompany a novel or poem.

GRAPHIC DESIGN
Industrialization and mass production began for graphic design in the mid-fifteenth century with the development of movable type, and was momentously marked by the printing of the Gutenburg Bible. For the first time in the Western world, instead of the painstaking hand-copying of books, many copies could be produced at once. The implications for communication are enormous. Literacy was a practical possibility for more than the privileged; ideas were freed from the few who, until this time, controlled the production and distribution of books.

For the pioneer printer, being a graphic designer was, no doubt, the least of his worries. He was beset by problems. In addition to designing his type, he had to learn how to cast it in metal, build presses, purchase paper, develop workable inks, sell his services, and frequently write the material to be printed. Through the sixteenth and seventeenth centuries the printers pushed forward, constantly improving their craft. Some of them have had their work immortalized by their type designers, many of them still used today, still identified by their creators' names, although it is often forgotten that these names refer to actual people—Bodoni, Garamond, Caslon—all printers who modestly plied their trade so long ago. Printing and the design of printed materials has always tended toward being a predominantly anonymous business.

The graphic designer as he exists today did not emerge until the true Industrial Revolution of the nineteenth century, when the refinement of printing and paper-making techniques made possible more creative decorative effects in the manipulation of text and illustration. It was the graphic artist and easel painter who turned his hand to the newly developed printing processes for creatively successful results. Toulouse-Lautrec was attracted by the poster format; William Morris, primarily an industrial designer, founded the Kelmscott Press; but these are exceptional instances. The forerunner of the graphic designer was a specialist in his work and usually labeled a "commercial artist," a title that contains overtones of condescension. The dedicated designer was rescued from the second-class citizenship to which the painters and critics relegated him. Led by the efforts of William Morris and then the Bauhaus, a new point of view developed—a resurgence of interest in the basic techniques of printing and an attempt to understand the capabilities of the processes and their various machinery that eventually resulted in the new look in printed matter. So often the "commercial artist" interpreted his assignment in a vacuum of ignorance of the mechanical process, leaving the printer with the unenviable job of adapting the artwork to a form that could be printed. Understanding between the two groups was at a low ebb.

With the newfound interest in the basic craft of printing, the designer has learned to work harmoniously with the printer, and this cooperation has been a prime factor in the improved quality of design in contemporary printing. In all of the graphic areas—design of typefaces, booklets, posters, packaging, letterheads, books—experimentation has led to powerful and dynamic results in more effective communication and also in attractiveness. The United States government has sent many exhibits of American graphics abroad, demonstrating the esteem shown for the quality of the work. The anonymous "commercial artist" of the past has been displaced by a highly imaginative graphic designer, whose name and style are honored by exhibit in those hallowed bastions of pure "Art"—the museums.

Although the thumbnail in graphic design is comparable to the sketch in painting and sculpture, it is more literal. It is useful to the designer in the preliminary search for possible solutions to a print piece, providing an opportunity for loose, probing variations and modifications on a single or a group of thematic visual paths. The thumbnail is self-descriptive; it is a miniature representation of the final piece. The smallness of the thumbnail offers the designer many special advantages that same-size sketches would not. For one thing you can do many of them, changing or discarding them easily since they can be done quickly. For another, thumbnails are simple to control, to keep neat, and to suggest what the solution will look like in its final form. There is one last value that miniaturization in thumbnails offers the

FIGURE 8.9

designer: in a very small area it is not only possible to try many different thumbnails, but, in the case of a booklet or a magazine with a number of pages the entire print piece can be seen at once as a whole, an effect that can be achieved only cumulatively in the sequential experience of the viewer (8.9). Total control of the whole through this method of previsualization means a designer has a stronger grasp on the total effect.

Going through the exercise of developing multiple solutions to one graphic design problem is a demonstration of relating the use of elements to character of the medium. In print, for instance, the dominating visual element is line; other elements, such as tone, color, texture, or scale, are secondary. The changes from one set of thumbnails to another offer the designer the choice of different visual techniques in a process of final determinations that clearly show the relationship between content and form. This relationship is especially crucial in the mass print media since they are a combination of words and pictures and abstract design formulation, and their basic nature is defined by their combination of the verbal and visual in a direct attempt to convey information.

From the thumbnail stage, choice of possible design solutions are usually narrowed down to two or three of the best thumbnails, and these are then translated in scale from the small version to the actual size the printed piece will be (8.10). This is a layout.

Each step of the way from the thumbnail to the final finished step requires some knowledge of the technical aspects of printing, such as typesetting, types of printing processes and their appropriateness for the project at hand, reproduction processes for the printing of all kinds of artwork from line drawings to black-and-white halftones to full-color plates. But even for the beginner who has the responsibility for the production of a poster or a booklet the key problem is the composition, the arrangement of the units of visual and verbal information that results in intended emphasis and clearly extended message. Printers can be very helpful with the technical solutions. With a background in visual literacy, a more educated effort can be applied to the design and production of print formats and, maybe even more importantly, to the understanding of the artistry or lack of it in the print messages we view.

FIGURE 8.10

CRAFTS

Craftsmen today occupy a special and esoteric place in society. Whatever they produce can probably be manufactured more quickly and
cheaply by a machine, but whether they can be made more artfully
is still a highly disputed question. In the past, the products made by
hand were an absolute necessity; in contemporary times, they are produced for people of special tastes, who can afford the increased cost
over the mass-produced product. Craftsmen have become "petits art-
istes," their work collected like paintings. There still exist lingering
echoes of the ideas of William Morris and his acolytes, who held that
without the individual touch of the craftsman there can be no beauty.
This protest against the machine and focus on the individual back-
fires at the other end, denying the whole rise in the standard of living
made possible by the Industrial Revolution. Mass production has
made the hand-made impractical, but it still has much to learn from
the craftsman and his knowledge of materials and how to work competently with them.

Each craft format has its own special characteristics of basic visual
elements, but all tend to be dominated by dimension and texture.
Planning for the production of a piece of handwoven cloth or a cera-
mic pot is not as rigorously detailed as it may be in other visual media. The solutions may be in the fingertips of the artist and arrived at
through actualized, one-to-one experimentation. Experience is also a
prime method for the evolution of a design in a slow progression of
production, allowing the artist to make minor modifications in newly
attempted pieces. If any techniques are dominant in the conception
and production of crafts, they are economy, simplicity, harmony.
But any craftsman, the serious and highly trained or the hobbyist,
must have an understanding of all aspects of visual literacy to be able
to grow toward technical and aesthetic development of expertise as
well as a firm control of medium and means.

The crafts—pottery, weaving, metal and woodworking of many varieties—in addition to being a means of supplying a market of specialized taste, have a growing appeal as a leisure activity. Many people
are turning to the crafts as a hobby, helping to stimulate a new and
lively interest in them.

INDUSTRIAL DESIGN

Unlike the devotees of the arts and crafts movement in England and

Europe, who turned their backs on the questionable standards of mass production, the Bauhaus group in Germany sought to understand the unique capabilities of the machine and searched for its unique capacity to produce objects embodying a new concept of beauty. The designer for industry became a contemporary craftsman and the word, "design," took on a new meaning—"the adaptation of a product to mass production." The Bauhaus philosophy did much to rescue the mass-produced from the tawdry copy of the hand-made: it inspired simple and functional products with a modern style. And nowhere in all the art movement has there been a more sincere interest in returning to the basics. The core program at the school led the students through "hands on" explorations of the essential qualities of the materials they worked with in much the same way that investigation of the basic visual components are recommended in the prusuit of visual literacy.

There have been many trends in industrial design for the mass production of furniture, clothes, automobiles, household equipment, tools, and so on. The most common is the purely functionalist approach which exposed elements of the basic structure as the predominant visual theme, resulting in an impersonal look, a neutrality of expression. Some efforts at industrial design resulted in a superstructure which ignored the inner workings of the product. The most glaring error of this sort was the design of the earliest streamlined engines for the Union Pacific Railroad. When the train was tested, it was discovered that the entire body of the engine would have to be lifted off every time it needed to be oiled. In fact, the whole idea of streamlining as a modern style spread from products intended for speed—automobiles, airplanes, boats—to many objects that were never destined to move.

To develop beautifully designed machinery and mass-produced artifacts, a fine balance between technical training and love of beauty must be developed and maintained. That is not easy. But immersion in the dynamic force of pure visual considerations is absolutely necessary for the technically trained, providing, as it does, an extension for understanding the problem at hand. Who, more than the engineer, can benefit from the abstract and conceptual quality of the visual component as viewed and defined in the context of visual literacy? The literal mind can only benefit from a point of view which hopes to move visual expression away from the orbit of intuition closer to an operational process of intellectual understanding and rational choices.

The most questionable factor in modern industrial design is obsolescence, the built-in perishability of appearance calculated to motivate an active turnover in production. Whether or not this practice contributes to sloppy workmanship, it does create a climate for accelerated fads in the appearance of products demanding more and more designers with constantly new ideas.

The constant change, no doubt, tests the mettle of the industrial designer. His work, if it is to be thought of as successful, must respond to the profit motive; he must see what he is designing as an element in the economical production of a salable product. It is difficult in this atmosphere to develop the integrity for making beautiful and functional products that the craftsman, with his intimate knowledge of materials and purpose, takes for granted. Businessmen are becoming more aware of how the successful design can increase sales. Ideally, the designer and the businessman must strike a balance. Walter Gropius expressed this need aptly in his 1919 comments on the aims of the Bauhaus: "Our ambition was to rouse the creative artist from his otherworldliness and to reintegrate him into the workaday world of realities and at the same time, to broaden and humanize the rigid, almost exclusively material mind of the businessman."

PHOTOGRAPHY
The development of photography was to the visual arts a complete revolution. The status of the artist and his relationship to society was completely upset; his irreplaceable uniqueness was forever altered by this new method of picture-making which could record infinite detail mechanically. The special talents and years of training that shaped and honed artistic skills were now challenged by a machine that could be operated by anyone within a comparatively short learning period. In the midst of our twentieth century and its overwhelming technological revolution which has produced unending electronic miracles, the photograph has come to be taken for granted. But the nineteenth century was still unsophisticated enough to be completely enthralled by the photograph.

First as a toy, then as a social necessity, the photograph served the middle class, its most devoted patron. It was not until the early twentieth century that the full impact of the photograph on communication became a reality. As Arthur Goldsmith put it aptly in his article, "The Photographer as a God," published in the magazine, Popular Photography,

"We live in an age dominated by photographs. In the invisible universe of men's minds and emotions, photography today exerts a force
comparable with the release of nuclear energy in the physical universe.
What we think, what we feel, our impressions of contemporary events
and recent history, our conceptions of man and the cosmos, the
things we buy (and don't buy), the pattern of our visual perceptions,
is shaped in some measure, and often decisively, by photography."

Making a record of family and friends and their activities is still the
major reason for the popularity of photography. The snapshot still re-
tains its enormous appeal and has been further developed by the invention by Edward Land of the Polaroid camera and film, which by-
passes the darkroom and produces instant pictures. From this great
army of photographers who use the camera for limited purposes
comes a continually growing group of serious amateurs, who study
the capabilities of the medium in greater depth, work in their own
darkrooms and hope to increase their creative aptitude. Some become professionals; most remain amateurs, contributing enormous
amounts of money and leisure time to what is, no doubt, the most
popular hobby in contemporary times.

But photography is also a profession of pivotal importance to the entire world of communication, a profession of many specializations.

The news photographer covers current events in a simple and direct
fashion. It is his job to produce bold, clear photographs which will retain their message despite the unsatisfactory reproduction of the
newspaper. The better reproduction capabilities of magazines offer
the photographer the opportunity for covering the same events in
greater depth with more subtlety. It was the technical strides of the
thirties which made the whole concept of the picture story possible,
first with better paper and printing methods, then with the miniature
camera and high-speed lenses, a revolution within a revolution which
freed the photographer of cumbersome equipment and, in bad light,
the annoyance of blinding flashbulbs. With a fast lens and fast film,
he could get in close enough to get the intimate picture, daring and
revealing, which brought history into our laps weekly.

The portrait photographer is still very much in business, unaffected
by the abundance of amateurs. His big studio cameras and retouching
skills supply the formal touch required by the undiminished demand
for the distinguished portrait that has survived down through the ages
of painters and daguerrotypists to the present. The documentary pho-

tographer, now frequently in the employ of industry or government, still works in the unchanged tradition of the past. And through microscopes, watertight cameras, special films, photography serves scientific experiment.

The photograph is dominated by the interactive visual element of tone/color although it also is composed of shape, texture, and scale. But photography also delivers to the artist and viewer the most convincing simulation of dimension, since the lens, like the human eye, sees and expresses what it sees in perfect perspective. Altogether the essential visual elements in the photograph replicate the environment and everything in it with enormous persuasion. The problem of the visual communicator is not to allow that power to dominate the design outcome, but rather to control it and bend it to the purpose and mood of the photographer. How? In the picture-taking process, imagination, the ability to previsualize, and "body English" combine to make possible for the photographer the same kind of unlimited options the designer-artist-synthesizer has available. It would appear the maker of pictures is limited by what is there in front of the camera and with the exception of a few controls of the information (smile, move a little to the left) must accept the circumstances. But this is a fallacy. One hundred photographers with cameras trained on the same subject will produce one hundred individual visual solutions in yet another predictable demonstration of the inevitable factor of subjective interpretation.

There are many variables available that offer a photographer a method for controlling the unyielding environmental information. First, and most important, is the expansion of visual concepts through exercises in visual literacy. Plans for a photograph or picture story can be put on paper—this is a good approach to preplanning. But it is likely the photographer will think visual images in the mind, see them on a mental screen. The compositional choices explored in sketch and plan must be achieved other ways. Squinting the eyes so as to reduce the visual information to simple, abstract shapes provides the compositional information that can be responded to and changed by crouching, bending, hopping on a chair, climbing a ladder. All these methods and gymnastics provide the photographer with the counterpart of the sketch in the previsualization process. The options can be expanded further by choices of type of camera, focal length of lenses, film (color or black and white), and time of day. One thing is certain —hardly any visual medium can be accomplished more easily, and so the opportunity for experimentation is both quick and inexpensive.

Since the very beginnings of this infant visual method, a few photographers have seen it as an art form and pursued it with no commercial purposes. In camera clubs, salons, international competitions, this artist-photographer has explored the possibilities of the camera in a totally creative manner. In recent times, such efforts have been recognized by exhibition and comparison to painting.

The photograph has one quality it shares with no other visual art—believability. The camera, the saying goes, cannot lie. Though this belief is highly questionable, it makes photography immeasurably potent in its ability to influence men's minds. Arthur Goldsmith, in the article previously quoted, comments on this pressing dilemma:

"One step toward a wiser, more useful application of photography's great power as a form of communication and art is a deeper understanding of the medium itself and how it acts on the human mind and emotions. But photography as a technique has tended to advance much more rapidly than have insights into the aesthetic and psychological implications of those techniques. In the long perspective of man's history, perhaps this is not surprising. If you used a yardstick to represent the span of time from Paleolithic cave paintings to the present, writing has existed for about six inches, but photography for a mere 1/8 inch! In that fraction of time we have only begun to understand the nature of the camera and its miracle."

FILM

If photography is represented by one-eighth of an inch in the span of visual history, then movies are just a speck. The experiments by Edison and the mechanical triumph of Lumière utilized the phenomenon of persistence of vision and made possible photographs that could record movement. Dramatic actions and events could be recorded and replayed any number of times. The early stages of experiment with this new medium had the virtue of built-in limitations (no color, no sound, no camera mobility) which broadened the basic knowledge of the filmmakers. Mime and exaggerated gesture compensated for the lack of dialogue. A slapstick humor, unique to the film, was brought to a point of perfection by the greatest movie clown, Chaplin. Documentary techniques expanded firsthand contact with a kind of living history book never before in any sense possible. Jean Cassou, in the essay, "Climate of Thought," from Gateway to the Twentieth Century, summed up the tremendous possibilities of the film:

"Thus the latest mechanical invention in the service of reality, destined subsequently to play its scientific role to such perfection, proved simultaneously to be an art possessing potentialities so immense and properties so unique that it not only embraced but surpassed all other arts. The cinema is at once an instrument of complete exactitude and a great poetical spellbinder: a mirror of truth, a dreamer of dreams and a worker of miracles."

The cinema had the same old pull between artistic expression and financial success. Making a movie, even the primitive one-reelers, required capital and with it a measure of control over the final product. Movies were, however, an instant and complete financial success. The public devoured them and enormous opportunities for expansion of the medium and experimentation in it were many. Eventually, full-length films with novel-like story lines emerged, along with that incomparable figure of modern times, the movie star. Sound was added and then color, and each was constantly improved. Movie-making became a major industry in which the big, expensive spectacle was associated with Hollywood and the more carefully budgeted creative efforts with Europe. Exceptions crisscross this fact the way, today, actors and production companies go back and forth across the Atlantic.

Both in the seeing and the making of films, the dominant visual element is movement. When this element is added to the realistic characteristics of the photograph, the result is the closest experience to what happens when we see. Of course, film can do much more than just replicate the human visual experience. It can carry information and deliver it in the most realistic manner. It can tell stories, collapsing time into a convention of its own. The magnitude of its power is the measure of how difficult it is to understand structurally, plan for, and control. Although verbal scripts are most often used to plan film projects, the visual quality of film is best dealt with through the use of a story board, a visual counterpart of the sketch or thumbnail (8.11). The storyboard, like the thumbnail, is also miniaturized and affords the filmmaker an opportunity to see the whole, or at least larger, segments than just individual shots and by doing so offers greater insight into the cumulative effect. It also provides the planner with an all-at-once control of the shot-by-shot interactive units of scenes in an overview of the entire design.

The storyboard also allows the film artist to incorporate the verbal material into the larger continuity design as well as music and, if they are to be used, sound effects. The segmented forces of film can be anticipated and controlled through the tentative, try-out solutions of the storyboard.

FIGURE 8.11

Increased technical knowledge widened the areas possible for moviemaking. Inexpensive cameras and film suited to the amateur were developed, and the counterpart of the snapshot, the home movie, was born. This amateur equipment, slightly refined, has been adopted by industrial and scientific filmmakers and is also suitable for the highly creative efforts of filmmakers who produce films as a personal and creative statement. Such work, artistic or documentary, is seen for the the most part in film festivals designed especially for them and on the increasingly expanded educational television stations. Even the commercial networks have been invaded by these expressive works and their stimulating and experimental techniques. In fact, television, an electronic medium divided between the use of live camera and films, once a seeming threat to the survival of the film, has done a great deal to expand public consciousness of the cinema. Frequent replays of old movies and the use of experimental short films have developed an audience of film buffs who regard the medium with a new seriousness that brings them back to the theater with more acute taste.

Still only an infant, film holds the promise of becoming a towering art form. Jean Cassou, in "Climate of Thought," sees the promise this way:

"The cinema, and only the cinema, with its mime and tempo, its technical constraints, its specific limitations, its fantastically fertile indigence, could have engendered the kind of laughter in which every class of society could participate, from those seeking only to laugh at the slightest opportunity to those demanding the satisfaction of subtle aesthetic demands. The absolute originality of the cinema—the "Seventh Art"—with its infinite potentialities was very clear from its earliest and most rudimentary productions. It must, however, be admitted, proclaimed even, that the development of the cinematographic art constitutes a remarkable adventure; that the cinema is, in fact, the characteristic, the great distinctive art form of the twentieth century."

TELEVISION

The concept of media in a modern sense is inextricably connected with the idea of mass audience. Strictly speaking, any message carrier—a wall painting, a speech, a personal letter—can be called a medium of communication. Such a reference would be valid, by definition, but today when we speak of media, it implies a large and possibly impersonal group of people "out there." It is in terms of group, or many groups, that mass messages are designed with the intention of winning response or cooperation from the audience.

Modern media, with their mass and unseen audience, are the collateral products of the Industrial Revolution and its capability for mass production. The hand-illuminated manuscripts of the Middle Ages would not qualify as media in this sense, nor would the epic poems of the Greeks, nor the ballads (and news, and opinions) of the wandering minstrels of Europe. Why? Individual variations not only could but probably would creep into the content. The end result would be that not every receiver of the information communicated could be guaranteed the identical message. This variation of basic message ended with the invention and the increasing use of movable

type. Once set in type, each separate copy of a printed piece is absolutely uniform, in fact, exactly alike. The idea of uniformity may not
be appealing. It has its good and bad aspects, but with it comes the inevitable outcome of the word <u>mass</u> in "mass media."

The book provoked and encouraged literacy, which broke the strangle-
hold on information held by the powerful and educated few. The
gathering, compilation, and distribution of information filtered down
to all levels of society in an Age of Enlightenment. The phenomenon
of the book is still with us. As the tribe, the village, the family yield-
ed to broader group identities and loyalties, the book and its parallel
print formats became the replacements for myth and symbol, fable
and morality play. What to do, what to think, what to know, how to
behave became a more public and uniform matter. Even now, in an era
dominated by electronic mass media, the book, and print in general,
are powerful agents of change. The key difference between the two
is <u>simultaneity</u>. The uniformity of mass-printed formats—books, magazines, newspapers, booklets, posters—makes the transmission of a
message to a large audience possible. But the advent of radio and television makes the same information and experience available to a mass
audience in the same instant.

The modern media have emerged from two parallel developments
that finally join. The first is the camera, the mechanical picture maker; the second is the radio waves' capability for transmitting data
over wire or through the atmosphere. The miracle of the camera,
which started with the camera obscura, the toy of the Renaissance,
did not end with fixed, preservable photographs. The camera obscura
could do something the camera could not: show movement. That
seemingly impossible accomplishment was realized through the slow
and painstaking efforts of many men, Muybridge, Edison, the Lumière brothers. Utilizing the phenomenon of persistence of vision, the
illusion of movement was replicated by the juxtaposition of impercep-
tively different pictures shown in rapid succession and regular sequence. The eye did the rest.

Together, the still photograph and the series of photographs that are
moving picture film, are only one path to the development of modern
mass media. The other is linked to the search for a means for sending
messages over long distances. The first method was the telegraph
(<u>tele</u>—the Greek prefix for "distant"), which sent a dot-dash audio
code over electric wires strung around the world, even under oceans

at the beginning of this century. But this invention of Samuel F. B. Morse was soon modified and refined into the telephone so it could carry more complex sounds. It was the capability for transmission of sound through space by means of electromagnetic waves that would, through the experiments of Scotchman Maxwell and German Hertz, form the beginnings of what would become radio. Just as Morse's telegraph, which transmitted sounds over wire, had suggested the telephone, which could transmit speech over the wire; so Marconi's wireless, which sent electric signals through the air, logically suggested the potential for sending articulated speech or other refined sounds such as music over the airwaves. This feat was first accomplished by an American, Reginald Aubrey Fessenden, in 1900.

Here the two paths join. Picture making and radio waves combine to create the most innovative and powerful of all modern media—television. The final steps of invention are complex and involved and enormously expensive: the selenium and mechanical disk, the cathode ray tube, the iconoscope, the kinescope. Each step was slow and halting, each involved contributions from many individuals. Limited programming started in the late thirties and early forties, but true television with network capability did not grow until after World War II.

The major difference in elemental terms between television and film is scale. All the other visual elements are the same. Film is intended to be seen larger than life, while television is the exact opposite. That is probably the chief reason for the more frequent utilization of the storyboard in the planning for a television presentation. Another motivating factor is that television is encompassed by ascribed time limitations. In planning for it, you not only have to know what is happening when, but exactly when and for exactly how long.

Visual choices for television are strongly influenced by the smallness of the screen and the distractions of the environment. These limitations make the need for clear and emphatic visual statement a priority. Against the distractions of people moving around, babies crying, phones ringing, the program planner must have a firm grasp of the counterforces of strong, dominant visual techniques starting with contrast and extending into exaggeration, accent, boldness, sharpness, and others that will reinforce the effects.

At this point in communication history, television can not only deliver the largest simultaneous audience of all time, but also, through the support of Telstar, can extend that audience beyond borders, beyond continents, beyond cultures. The implications are staggering. The historic moments of man can be shared wherever there is television broadcast anywhere in the world. Conversely, the events which might have been removed from direct experience, even muted, are looked at through the unrelenting, the penetrating eye of the camera. True, the aural-visual content of television can be controlled, even manipulated. But complaints that film or television can distort information any more than any other media are unjustified. What probably engenders the defensiveness is the pure power of pictures and words that television can deliver with such intimate and privileged quality (8.12). The tar paper shacks of the rural South saw through television a world they never imagined. So did the slum dwellers of the North.

FIGURE 8.12

The results should not surprise anyone! A whole nation of Americans watched nightly the film reports on a distant war being fought by their sons. An entirely new response to war has emerged from the experience. Political conventions, popular heroes, riots and entertainment, all are being seen, if not in the moment, then close. The lone television set in village of Brazil or Ghana broadcasting a dubbed version of "I Love Lucy" or the "Virginian" is commonplace. The chant can go up: "The whole world is watching," watching themselves, watching each other; and the result holds profound power over social change.

There are many lesser formats of the visual arts than could possibly be covered here; many of them little practiced or recognized, such as lighting design, interior decoration, type design. For all the natural and appropriate visibility they have, we may not be aware of how they pervade our experience and life style: the enormous world of political cartoons, the comic strips, the restless and ever-changing fashions of clothes design. All are, in some part, variations and combinations of the visual mode that influence every aspect of the environment. In fact, one of the emerging formats is an offshoot of city planning called environmental design. We live with them in such proximity, but do we notice them? We may indeed ask, "How many see?"

But in the future, there will no longer be artists as we have known them and as the modern world has defined them. The very forces that first inspired man to fulfill his needs and express his ideas through visual means are no longer just the province of the artist. Even the most sophisticated picture making, thanks to the camera, is, technically, possible for anyone. But technics are not enough, nor artistic intuition, nor cultural conditioning. To understand visual media, to express ideas in visual terminology, it will be necessary to study the components of visual intelligence, the basic elements, the syntactical structures, the perceptual mechanisms, the techniques, the styles and systems. By studying them, we can control them as man has learned to understand, control, and use language. Then, and only then, will we achieve visual literacy.

9
VISUAL LITERACY:
HOW AND WHY

The world did not arrive at a high level of verbal literacy quickly or easily. In many countries it is not yet a viable reality. The problem is no different for visual literacy. Right at the core of the problem of visual literacy is a paradox. Much of the process is already a capability of sighted, intelligent people. How many see? Ostensibly everyone but the blind. How can you study what you already know? The answer to this question lies in a definition of visual literacy as more than just seeing, more than just making visual messages. Visual literacy implies understanding, the means for seeing and sharing meaning with some level of predictable universality. To accomplish this requires reaching beyond the innate visual powers of the human organism, reaching beyond the intuitive capabilities programmed into us for making visual decisions on a more or less common basis, and reaching beyond personal preference and individual taste.

A verbally literate person is defined as one who can read and write, but this definition can be extended to mean an educated person. For visual literacy the same extension of meaning should hold true. Beyond providing a body of shared information and experience, visual literacy holds a promise of an educated understanding of that information and experience. When you note the many concepts that are necessary to achieve visual literacy, the complexity of the endeavor should be abundantly obvious. Unfortunately, there is no shortcut to follow through the multiple definitions and characteristics in the visual vocabulary that can take us to an easy point of clarification and control. There are plenty of simple formulas; they abound in how-to-do-it books. But they tend to be one dimensional, thin and limiting, and do not represent the most desirable quality of the visual means, its limitless descriptive power and its infinite variety. There is little reason to complain about the complexity of visual expression when you realize and value its richness.

The point that language is not analogous to visual literacy has been made many times for differing reasons. But language is a means of expression and communication and, therefore, is a parallel system to visual communication. We cannot slavishly copy the methods that are used to teach reading and writing, but we can observe and acknowledge them. To learn to read and write, you start at the base elemental level by learning the alphabet by rote. This method is reflected by a similar approach to becoming visually literate. Each of the simplest units of visual information, the elements, should be explored and learned from every point of view of their quality and character and expressive potential. The process shouldn't aim at being any faster than learning the ABCs. Because visual information is more complicated and broader in its definitions and associative in its meanings, it should, if anything, take longer to learn. At the end of a long period of involvement and exposure to the visual elements, the results should reflect what it means when we finally learn the whole alphabet. There should be an intimate familiarity with the visual elements. We should know them "by heart." In other words the recognition or use of them should be escalated to a higher plateau of knowing that incorporates them into the unconscious as well as conscious mind for almost automatic access. They should be there but not intrusively, noted but not sounded out as beginning readers sound out individual letters when they read.

The same intensive method of exploration should be applied to the compositional stage of visual input or output. Composition is primarily influenced by the diversity of forces implicit in the psychophysiological factors of human perception. They are givens on which the visual communicator can depend. Awareness of visual substance is perceived not only through seeing but through all of the senses, and it provides not isolated individual pieces of information but whole interactive units, totalities which through sight and perception we assimilate directly and with great speed. The process provides the understanding of how the organization of a mental image and the structuring of a composition happens and how, once having happened, it functions.

The entire process can be applied to any visual problem. The guidelines presented in psychology, particularly Gestalt psychology, complement the utilization of visual techniques in arriving at an interpretation of an idea in a composition. Whether in sketching or photography or interior design, much of the control of final results lies in the manipulation of the elements by the intricate mechanism of visual techniques. Familiarity through use and observation of each of the techniques releases the wide range of effects made possible by their subtle steps from polarity to polarity. The range of options is enormous; the choices multiple.

Compositional wholes along with the choices of techniques and their relative importance are a vocabulary of expression that corresponds to the structural arrangements and words in verbal literacy. Deeper investigation and knowledge of both will open more doors to understanding and controlling of the visual means. It takes time. We must examine our methods with the same rigor we apply to language or mathematics or any other universally shared system that holds meaning.

Somehow, for some reason or numbers of reasons, the visual mode is considered either totally beyond the control of the untalented or, conversely, immediately—if not instantly—obtainable. The assumed ease in visual expression may be connected to the naturalness of seeing or possibly to the instant quality of the camera. Surely the whole point of view is reinforced by the lack of methodology for achieving visual literacy. Whatever the exact sources, both assumptions are false and probably responsible for the low quality of visual product in so many media of visual expression. Educators must respond to all those who need to expand their visual literacy capability. They must bring themselves to the point of realization that visual expression is neither appropriate for custodial playtime nor esoteric, mystical magic. Then there would be a fair chance of introducing a course of study that views all educated people as able to be as visually literate as they are verbally literate.

A methodology is important; deep immersion in the elements and techniques is vital; a slow step-by-step process is in order. Such an approach can open doors to understanding and control of the visual means. But the road is long and the process slow. How many years does it take for a child or adult who can speak perfectly well to learn to read and write? Beyond that, how does familiarity with the tool of verbal literacy affect control of written language as a medium of expression? Time and involvement, analysis and practice, all are necessary to tie intention and result in both the verbal and visual mode. In both cases, it is a scale on which we may score differently, but literacy means an ability to express and understand, and in both the verbal and the visual the ability can be learned by everyone. And should be.

This quality of engagement, of overcoming the limitations falsely imposed on visual expression, is absolutely essential in pursuit of visual literacy. Opening up the educational system to include visual literacy or responding to individual curiosity is a strong first step. Or it can be done by anyone who feels the need to expand their own potential for enjoyment of the visual from subjective expression to practical application. It is, as noted, complex, but it is not mysterious. From individual data to a broad view of the media you must think about it, observe it in depth where you experience it, see how others accomplish their purposes, and try it yourself.

What are the advantages for nonartists in developing their visual acuity and expressive potential? The first and crucial value lies in the development of criteria that extend beyond natural response and personal or conditioned tastes and preferences. Only those who are visually sophisticated can rise above fashion and fad to make their own choices and judgments of what is appropriate and aesthetically pleasing. At a slightly higher level of involvement, visual literacy offers a command of the mode, control of the effects. Literacy means participation and makes those who have achieved it less passive observers. In effect, visual literacy precludes the "Emperor's clothes" syndrome and makes of judgment a higher action than acceptance (or rejection) of a visual statement based on intuition alone. Visual literacy means increased visual intelligence.

This makes visual literacy a practical concern for the educator. Increased visual intelligence means easier understanding of all meaning which takes visual form. Visual decisions dominate a great deal of what we examine and recognize even in reading. For too long the importance of this simple fact has been neglected. Visual intelligence increases the effect of human intelligence, extends the creative spirit. It is not only a necessity but, happily, a promise of human enrichment in the future.

BIBLIOGRAPHY

Anderson, Donald M., Elements of Design. New York: Holt, Rinehart, Winston, 1961.

Arnheim, Rudolf, Art and Visual Perception. Berkeley, Calif.: University of California Press, 1954.

Berenson, Bernard, Seeing and Knowing. Greenwich, Conn.: New York Graphic Society, 1969.

Cassou, Jean; Langui, Emil; and Pevsner, Nikolaus, Gateway to the Twentieth Century. New York: McGraw-Hill, 1962.

Collingwood, R. G., The Principles of Art. New York: Galaxy Books, Oxford University Press, 1958.

de Sausmarez, Maurice, Basic Design: The Dynamics of Visual Form. New York: Reinhold, 1969.

Ehrenzweig, Anton, The Hidden Order of Art. Berkeley, Calif.: University of California Press, 1967.

Gattegno, Caleb, Towards a Visual Culture: Educating through Television. New York: Outerbridge and Dienstfrey, 1969.

Gombrich, E. H., The Story of Art, 11th ed. New York: Phaedon, 1966.

Gregory, Richard L., The Intelligent Eye. New York: McGraw-Hill, 1970.

Hogg, James, ed., Psychology and the Visual Arts. Baltimore, Md.: Penguin, 1970.

Ivins, William M., Jr., Prints and Visual Communication. London: Routledge & Kegan Paul, Ltd., 1953; Cambridge, Mass.: The MIT Press, 1969.

Koestler, Arthur, The Act of Creation. New York: Macmillan, 1964.

Koffka, K., Principles of Gestalt Psychology. New York: Harbinger Book, Harcourt, Brace and World, 1935.

Langer, Susanne K., Philosophy in a New Key. New York: Mentor, New American Library, 1957.

Langer, Susanne K., Problems of Art. New York: Scribner's, 1957.

Langer, Susanne K., ed., Reflections on Art. New York: Galaxy Books, Oxford University Press, 1961.

Pevsner, Nikolaus, Pioneers of Modern Design. Baltimore, Md.: Pelican, Penguin, 1964.

Read, Herbert, The Grass Roots of Art. New York: Meridian Books, World Publishing, 1961.

Read, Herbert, The Meaning of Art. Baltimore, Md.: Pelican, Penguin, 1961.

Ross, Ralph, Symbols and Civilization. New York: Harbinger Book, Harcourt, Brace and Johanovich, 1963.

Vernon, M. D., ed., Experiments in Visual Perception. Baltimore, Md.: Penguin, 1962.

White, Lancelot Law, ed., Aspects of Form. Bloomington, Ind.: Indiana University Press, 1961.

Wind, Edgar, Art and Anarchy. New York: Vintage Books, Random House, 1969.

ILLUSTRATION CREDITS

The numbers in parentheses following the figure numbers are the page numbers on which the figures appear. All figures are reproduced with permission.

Jacqueline Casey of the MIT Publications Office designed the posters and announcements which are reproduced as Figures 6.8c (113), 6.12b (115), 6.13b (115), 6.14b, c (116), 6.15c (116), 6.19b (118), 6.22b, c (119), 6.25b (120), 6.26b (120), 6.27c (121), 6.29c (122), 6.30c (122), 6.36b, c (125), and 6.38c (125).

Ralph Coburn of the MIT Publications Office designed the posters and announcements which are reproduced as Figures 6.4b, c (111), 6.6b, c (112), 6.8b (113), 6.9c (113), 6.17c (117), 6.18b, c (117), 6.23b (119), 6.24c (120), 6.25c (120), 6.26c (120), 6.28b, c (121), 6.32b, c (123), and 6.41b, c (126).

The photograph, Figure 8.3 (154), is by Waldo.

Carl Zahn of the Museum of Fine Arts, Boston, designed the graphic material reproduced as Figures 6.11b (114), 6.15b (116), 6.16b (116), 6.31c (122), 6.33c (123), and 6.40b, c (126).

The drawing and the photograph of the model of Boston City, Hall, Figures 3.12 (43) and 3.47 (63), are reproduced courtesy of the architects, Kallman, Knowles, and McKinnell.

Figures 4.2 (70), 4.3 (71), 4.12 a (75), 4.12 b, c (76), 4.13 a, b, c (77), 5.13 (95), 5.14 (95), and 7.1 (130) are reproduced courtesy of the Museum of Fine Arts, Boston.

The author provided the material for Figures 3.11 (43), Plate 3.1 (53), Figures 3.45 (62), 3.46 (63), 4.1 (70), 5.27 (102), 5.28 (102), 5.29 (102), 6.10c (114), 6.11c (114), 6.12c (115), 6.13c (115), 6.19c (118), 6.20c (118), 6.21b (118), 6.24b (120), 6.29b (122), 6.30a (122), 6.33b (123), 6.34b, c (124), 6.35b (124), 6.37b (125), 6.38b (125), 6.39b (126), 7.2 (131), 7.4 (135), 7.5 (137), 7.6 (139), 7.7 (141), 7.8 (143), 8.1 (152), 8.7 (162), 8.8 (162), 8.9 (166), 8.10 (168), 8.11 (176), and 8.12 (180). The sculpture pictured in Figures 3.45 and 3.46 is by Emory Goff and is in the collection of the author.

Figures 8.2 (153) and 8.4 (156) are taken from the Sketchbooks of Leonardo Da Vinci.

Figures 6.5b (112), 6.7c (112), 6.9b (113), 6.10b (114), 6.17b (117), 6.20b (118), 6.23c (119), 6.27 (121), 6.30b (122), 6.31b (122), 6.35c (124), 6.37c (125), 6.39c (126), 8.5 (157), and 8.6 (158) are reproduced from books and announcements published by The MIT Press. The cover, Figure 6.7b (112), was designed for the MIT Press by Bernie LaCasse.

Figures 4.20 (80), 4.21 (80), 4.22 (81), and 6.31a (122) were student exercises.

INDEX

.